W9-CTD-941

POST traumatic QUEST

My Quest to Transcend Trauma,
Turn My Pain Into Purpose, and Find Peace

Danny Sanchez

A Memoir
with Abigail Reynaga Sanchez

This book is memoir. It reflects the author's present recollections of experiences over time. Some names and characteristics have been changed, some events have been compressed, and some dialogue has been recreated.

Post Traumatic Quest, LLC
6017 Snell Ave #460
San Jose, CA 95123
posttraumaticquest.com

ISBN 978-1-7367779-0-9 (hardcover)
ISBN 978-1-7367779-1-6 (paperback)
ISBN 978-1-7367779-2-3 (e-Book)

Cover Illustration by Elba Raquel (elbaraquel.com)
Cover design and logo by Tosh Woods

Dedication

This book is dedicated in loving memory to Grandpa and Grandma, Dr. Don and Ruthanne Phillips, true examples of faith, hope, and love. Thank you for investing in me and loving me unconditionally. I am forever grateful.

Preface

It is scary to bare your soul and sins. I hope that making myself vulnerable in this way can be of some help to those who can relate. Some will relate on a personal, first-hand level. I hope those who don't will gain a better understanding for struggling youth they encounter acting out in destructive ways, like I was. There is always more to the story and something deeper going on underneath that behavior.

I can't share my story without mentioning family members and figures in my life. I bring them up not to judge or blame them in any way. Memories are imperfect. My opinions and perceptions are my own. Mainstream culture, social norms, ways of life, and we as individuals change throughout the years.

We are all on a different journey and have different beliefs. I know everyone has their own definition of a "higher power," if they choose to believe in one. For me, it's been my faith in Jesus Christ.

I believe we can all relate to each other through love and empathy, despite different beliefs and backgrounds.

My story may be triggering for some people. I talk about abuse and violence I witnessed and endured.

I'm ashamed to say I did many things I regret and hurt many people. I can't change the past, but I pray my mistakes can be turned around and used for good in some way, whether to prevent others from making the same mistakes, give hope to those who have, or offer empathy and understanding to those living a similar lifestyle.

Table of Contents

CHAPTER 1

Life Is Like a Mist

"Yet you do not know what tomorrow will bring. What is your life? For you are a mist that appears for a little time and then vanishes."

James 4:14 ESV

Even though I was fascinated with death, I didn't actually consider the afterlife until the day I faced it for real.

When I was twenty-four, I decided to become a Christian, and it was the worst experience of my life.

That journey began with my friend A.V. and me in the parking lot of The Rock Garden music studio in downtown San Jose, California. Our band would often practice there. We had just wrapped up practicing one of our latest songs. We were drunk and looking for trouble. We started arguing with some guy there and it quickly escalated to a fight between him and A.V. They chased each other across the street and over a chain link fence. The next thing I knew, A.V. was flat on the ground, and it didn't look good. I sprinted over to help him.

The guy started hitting at my hands as I grabbed onto the fence to climb it. Once I jumped over, I felt him punching me sharply on my upper body. My hands felt slippery and useless. I looked down to see blood running out of deep gouges in my arms. I hadn't realized this guy was stabbing me with some kind of a dull garden tool he had on him. A.V. had been stabbed too. He managed to get off the ground where he was lying and hit the guy hard, knocking him down.

I was furious that I had been stabbed. Adrenaline and hot anger pumped through me. I snatched the metal utensil away from my adversary, and, in a fit of rage, I stabbed him repeatedly. Luckily, we heard a siren before any life-threatening damage occurred.

I tried to escape by jumping the fence, but I couldn't pull myself up. A.V. tried to help me over, but I could barely lift my arms above my head, let alone lift my body weight. My muscles were torn and severed from deep puncture wounds. Although my blood was pumping hard and I was full of energy, my arms were like jelly. A.V. fled the scene just in time. I was caught.

I was taken by ambulance to the hospital and wheeled into Emergency. Guess who was just behind the curtain on the other side of my room? The garden tool maniac. We continued our fight, only verbally now, yelling at each other from our gurneys. Somehow, he was allowed to go home after treatment, and I was taken to jail. At the time, I thought this was so unfair because he had stabbed me first, more times than I had stabbed him.

I should have been kept in the infirmary, but I was made to stay in the old jail (the main jail downtown). I was in constant, agonizing pain for many weeks. My wounds were open holes that could not be stitched up. The only remedy was to prevent infection by washing them out with saline water. I dreaded this every time, because it burned so badly, and my arms would throb for hours afterward. I couldn't find a comfortable position at night on my bunk and didn't get much sleep for over a month. I would go the infirmary every day to ask for pain medication, but they wouldn't give me anything. To this day, I have ugly scars, a severed muscle on my right side, and numb spots on my hands and arms.

I was so miserable and sick of my life that I called my uncle Eddy, who was a pastor at a church in San Jose. I was in a desperate place and willing to try anything. He wrote me a letter, and I decided to become a Christian. I started attending Bible studies during my six-month stay in jail. The main shot caller there for the Mexicans was good people. He actually supported my decision to follow Christianity, but there was hell to pay from everyone else.

I didn't have to do the program (prison gangs each have their own rules including workout routines and schedules). I really couldn't have followed the program anyway with my injuries. Everyone else had to wake up early each morning and work out, and they didn't like the fact that I didn't. I usually thrived in jail, but being there as a "Christian" was demeaning. I was now an outcast.

Everything I did was carefully watched and scrutinized. They were waiting for me to fall and provoking me to fight because they knew I wasn't supposed to now. Day after day I was mocked with no one to back me up. I used to enjoy the social status I had in jail, but now I was on the very bottom and I hated it. On top of all that, I was in so much pain. I sunk into depression, questioning why God would put me through this. I didn't recognize my long history of bad decisions. I had a pattern of blaming others and seeing myself as the victim.

The first thing I did upon my release was buy a forty ounce of malt liquor and put my Christian days behind me. If that was what it was like to be Christian, then I wanted nothing to do with it. I guess in some ways my conversion was an attempt at an easy way out. My own pride still ruled my heart. I believed things should immediately go my way, that God should give me what I wanted instead of me doing things His way or seeking His will.

At that point in my life, I was so depressed I didn't feel like living. I had always had a feeling that I had been dodging death my entire life. When I was a teenager, I dared death to take me down. Today I encounter it head on. I work, quite literally, in the shadow of death, going into gang hot spots as I meet with families after gang-related homicide. I conduct funerals attended by many gang members, all of which could become dangerous in an instant.

It is said life is like a vapor or a mist, here one minute and gone the next. I know this to be true. I have attended and conducted many funerals throughout my forty-eight years of life. I was in the room while a beautiful two-year-old baby girl took her last breath in her mother's arms, and I have given the eulogy for a one-hundred-and-six-year-old woman and many others in between. I myself should have died countless times, and everyone who knew me thought so too.

When I was a one-year-old baby in my crib, my four-year-old brother grabbed my dad's loaded pistol and shot a hole in our bedroom wall. My dad and his friends were downstairs in the basement tending to their marijuana plants when the shot and my cries echoed through the house. Incredibly, both my brother and I were unharmed.

In the early 1980s, my dad would take us to his friend's ranch in the Evergreen foothills in San Jose where we would play outside all day with his friend's two boys. One morning when I was about eight and my brother was about eleven, my dad took out his shotgun. He aimed and fired at a watermelon. As the melon exploded in front of us, my father asked, "Do you want your brother's head to look like that?" We looked at each other wide eyed and shook our heads no. "Well then don't point the gun at your brother." That was the entirety of our gun safety lesson.

He then gave us each a .22 shotgun and let us run wild on the ranch, shooting whatever we wanted. It's a wonder we didn't all kill each other. One night when my older brother was only eleven, he drove us home because my dad was passed out in the van, and we didn't want to stay the night there.

When I was sixteen, two men tried to kill me by throwing me off the indoor balcony at the Embassy Suites Hotel in Milpitas, California. I was at a party there, and as usual, I got into a fight. The two guys I was fighting with cornered me against the railing and tried to push me over. I was clinging onto the rail and kicking down as they grabbed my legs, trying to pick me up and throw me off of the eighth floor. Just as I was losing my grip, my cousin came out of the hotel room and saved me at the last second.

Several years later, when I was on the fifth tier of San Quentin State Prison, I would be reminded of that moment. The walkway covering all four walls had a lot of similarities to that balcony, and when you are up there walking behind the guardrail or standing at the top of the steep cement stairs looking down, you know that all it takes is one push. Everyone walked around acting hard because we knew how fragile we really were. In a split second, a kneejerk reaction, your freedom can be taken away, your life lost, or someone else's.

In my early twenties, I was in a high-speed car accident on the 101 freeway. The vehicle rolled eight times. I just remember seeing dirt, sky, dirt, sky, and hearing moans from my friend as his body was impacted on each spin. We were told that the only reason the car didn't explode into flames was because the gas tank was practically empty. I was fine, other than being pretty banged up and bruised, with a huge mark from the seatbelt across my chest.

It is amazing I survived my childhood, but my later years were even worse.

As I got older, I chose over and over to put my own life at risk. I was crying out for someone to help me. I wanted to be noticed and cared for, but it seemed to me that nothing I did was enough for someone to step in. I felt ignored. I guess I wanted someone to tell me they would be devastated if I was gone. Instead, my dangerous behavior just pushed everyone away. My family has told me that they always expected a phone call saying I was dead.

The scary thing is that death doesn't only come to the risk-takers like me. Any of us can go at any time. We don't like to think about that, but every time I am at a funeral, I see this realization in people's eyes. "It could be me." Personally, this thought didn't bother me. I had no peace in my life, so I was intrigued by death and flirted with it for many years. I romanticized death, completely missing the point of living life for a purpose. **Even though I was fascinated with death, I didn't actually consider the afterlife until the day I faced it for real.**

"And as it is appointed for men to die once, but after this the judgment, so Christ was offered once to bear the sins of many."

Hebrews 9:27–28

CHAPTER 2

Hunger for a Solid Home

Everyone seemed to have a place except for me.

I was born to Raul "Roy" and Gloria. My parents were married in 1970 on my father's eighteenth birthday. My mother was also eighteen. Three months after they were married, my older brother Roy Jr. was born. Three years later, I was born, little Danny boy, at Alexian Brothers Catholic Hospital in East San Jose. Today it is called Regional Hospital. San Jose has been my lifelong home, and my family has deep roots here. I was baptized at Most Holy Trinity Church near Overfelt High School when I was a few months old.

Mom and Dad

I can't remember much of life together as a family. What I do remember from that time is crouching in terror in the closet while my dad beat my mom with a leather belt, spanking her and demeaning her. He would often humiliate my mom. One time when she didn't make his eggs the way he liked, he threw the plate, breaking it and making a big mess for her to clean up.

When I was about three, my dad got another girl pregnant. I remember seeing my mom throwing all my dad's things out the front door. I now understand it was because he was cheating on her, but as a child, I always resented her for making my dad leave. He ended up divorcing my mom and marrying the other woman. I just wanted them to get back together. I felt my family had been ripped apart, and I could never know who I would lose next.

My mom, my older brother Roy, and I moved to my grandparents' house. Grandpa Pete and Grandma Julia provided a solid home for us. They were actually my great-grandparents; my mom was born to their teenage daughter. They raised my mom and her cousin Eddy as their children. After raising two generations and now a third, they were tired. My grandfather was too old to want to be bothered with me. He would yell at us in Spanish, but I didn't know what he was saying. Other than that, he ignored us. For the most part, my presence seemed to irritate him.

Both of my parents speak Spanish, but they grew up in a time when kids were punished for using it in the classroom. As a result, it wasn't something that was passed down to me. Spanish was prevalent in my neighborhood and even in my home, but I didn't understand it at all.

Grandpa Pete was king of his house. When he dressed up, he wore a fedora hat. That look is how we all remember him now, in his sharp suit and dark fedora hat. Back then, we all tried to avoid doing anything to set off his temper. Grandma served him hand and foot.

My grandmother Julia worked tirelessly taking care of the house and everyone in it. She was fast and efficient at everything she did, whipping up homemade tortillas with a quick roll and pat.

The freshest tortillas hot off the stove were for my grandpa. The tortillas from earlier in the day or the day before were for the rest of us. I would point meekly to the warm tortillas, knowing they were supposed to be for grandpa. She would hesitate for a split second, then slap on butter as she handed me the hot tortilla in one swift motion, with the butter immediately melting on contact. I would gobble it up, feeling like I had scored a secret prize.

There was always a warm pot of beans on the stove. I loved eating her papas con carne (meat in red sauce with potatoes). It was my staple food. I loved it so much that even when my mom asked what I wanted to eat on my birthday, thinking I would ask for McDonald's or something special, all I wanted was papas con carne.

Grandma could whip up a hot meal on a moment's notice, and it was consistently delicious. Everything was always piping hot and fresh off the stove. To this day, I can't stand my food or coffee to be less than scalding hot. Grandma was constantly cooking and cleaning and sometimes even gardening. She would put on her gardening gloves and grab her pruning shears to tend to her roses. She had beautiful roses all along the perimeter of the front yard, and she had a white picket fence. Sometimes on hot days, she would let us run through the sprinklers in our chonies or bring out a little plastic pool.

Playing in my grandma's front yard. Me and Mom.

The backyard was Grandpa's domain. He had a rabbit pen full of rabbits. There were wood piles, tools, cactus plants, and a work shack. We would play, dig holes, and run around getting filthy. Grandma would send us straight to the bath to wash up. Sometimes she was a little rough when scrubbing our faces in a hurry or combing our hair, but her hugs were warm when I was sleepy or hurt. I could always run into her arms.

Most evenings my uncle would come over after work, and we would all sit around the fireside in the living room. Roy and I would sit on the floor as close as we could stand and poke sticks into the fireplace watching them catch flame. Grandpa kept a careful eye on us but let us have our fun. We felt like men being allowed to handle the fire. Sometimes Grandpa would let us pull some wood from the pile in the backyard and throw it in ourselves, while he sat and watched Lawrence Welk.

Visits with my dad were the complete opposite. There were tons of people hanging out partying all the time. There would be burnt spoons laying around from cooking-up, and smoke-filled rooms. We kids would have to sit around for hours or find our own sources of entertainment. We climbed trees, climbed the roof, rode minibikes, played with bows and arrows, and were part of all kinds of crazy activities. We didn't have any rules except to stay out their hair.

It was fun when they would take their parties to a park and we could run around there. We usually went to Welch Park in East San Jose, off Tully Road. We would roll up in low rider cars with ice chests full of Budweiser. They were decked out in pendletons and bandanas with their big brush mustaches. Oldies would be blasting as they passed around joints. I remember one barbeque at Hellyer park—I think I was about nine—my uncle dared me to eat a jala-peño. He said he would give me five bucks if I ate the whole thing. I prepared myself for the worst and tried to get it over with as fast as I could, but I discovered I actually liked it. It began my life-long love affair with spicy food, and to top it off, I got five dollars.

Going back and forth between my dad and my mom was hard on me. My dad started a new family with his new wife when my sister Angie was born. I had a nagging sense of abandonment. **Everyone seemed to have a place except for me.** All my life, I did dangerous and crazy things because of this empty, unwanted feeling. I wanted to know I was really special to them and always would be, but I felt like I was just an annoyance.

CHAPTER 3

Labeled a Loser

I would act out constantly in the hope that people would see me as funny or even bad, as long as they didn't notice I was dumb.

Living at my grandparents' provided security for us, but emotionally I was anxious, especially at bedtime.

My mom had a very hard life. After my dad left, she had to raise two young boys alone. She often worked nights. She would set my clothes out before she left so Grandma wouldn't have to fuss with that in morning. My outfit would be hanging up ready for me when I woke up. She always dressed us nice, somehow, even on little money.

While she slept during the day, I played quietly with my G.I. Joes and dinosaurs and pretended that her quilted body was a mountain range with caves and valleys. I could play by myself for hours, swept away by my imagination. It was lonely but peaceful. I liked the quiet time alone with my mom, even if she was mostly sleeping. When I was hungry, I would grab a package of my favorite food, Sopas (Sopa de Conchitas), and stand by my sleeping mother, wishing she would just know I was there so I wouldn't have to wake her.

Eventually, she got a day job working hard and liked to go dancing with her friends at night. Every day I would stare out the window longing for her to come home. Then at night I would lock my arms around her in a death grip, willing her not to leave while I slept. She was my whole world and security. I didn't want to lose her the way I lost my dad.

Looking back now, I think my grandparents wanted her to put us to bed before she could go out. She would lay down with me to try to get me to fall asleep. I would muster all my strength to cling to my mother's arm as tightly as I could. I was determined to never let go. I would drift off to sleep envisioning Mom walking around at the discotheque with me, her four-year-old son, dragging from her wrist. But when I woke up in the morning, she would be gone. I thought if I begged, cried, and clung to her I could make her stay. When I woke up alone, I knew I had no control over what happened to me, and I didn't feel truly safe. It was an insecure, uneasy feeling that stayed with me. I was afraid of being alone.

One time while I was waiting impatiently for mom to come home, Roy thought it would be funny to lie and tell me she was driving up. I ran out the front door as fast as I could. I stopped, puzzled. Roy started cracking up and called me a baby. I grabbed the first thing I saw when I chased him back into the house: a pen. I was so mad I stabbed him in the arm and broke the skin.

Mom always tried her best to give me everything I wanted. Even though we didn't have much money, she made sure we had the same clothes and toys as everyone else so we wouldn't feel less than. Whenever I cried for something in the store, Mom would give it to me so I would be quiet. Yes, I was a spoiled brat, throwing tantrums to get my way.

Once when I was crying for a Spiderman action figure in Kmart that Mom didn't have the money to buy, she just shoved it into her purse to shut me up. I learned to equate gifts, more than anything else, with love. I also craved physical affection. Gifts and affection were the only way I felt loved. I wanted all the cool toys and clothes. My identity was wrapped up in what I owned. I was trained to believe that it wasn't about how much money you saved or whether or not you worked hard to make an honest living. Looking the part was what mattered. It was always about how much we could get, never about giving back.

When my mom was home and exhausted, I would attempt to get her attention by irritating her. As I got older, my behavior grew increasingly annoying, so Mom would yell and hit me. Now I know she was probably hungover at times and not in the mood for my antics. To me it seemed like she was grumpy and mad at me all the time, so I would act out even more. One time she was hitting me with a belt so badly that my brother Roy jumped on top of me to protect me.

When my little brother was born, I became the middle child and felt even more out of place. I did things to make my mom mad, and then I would feel unloved and believe she loved my other brothers more. That made me do more horrible things, which then reinforced my belief. I would repeat this cycle over and over with my family, and in romantic relationships as well, looking for attention in unhealthy ways.

My dad never seemed to care about what I did. I learned that the word "no" simply meant to keep on whining until I got my way. Maybe that's why I never thought mom would really follow through on sending me to kindergarten. On the first day of school, I begged and wailed to stay home. When I was eventually peeled off my mother and pushed through the door of the classroom, I was in shock, crushed, and unable to believe she actually did it. I had thrown the mother of all tantrums, but I was still forced to go to school. I was learning I couldn't count on a certain response or be sure of what to expect. It was a helpless feeling.

School introduced a whole new set of problems. There I learned about failure and defeat. It was difficult for me to sit and pay attention in class. I needed one-on-one attention in order to understand things, but because I was so unruly, no teacher wanted to help me.

I was frustrated because I simply couldn't do what was expected of me. I was behind in class, and when I got home, no one had time to help me with my homework. Homework didn't even cross our minds. I was always in trouble. I felt stupid and embarrassed. **I would act out constantly in the hope that people would see me as funny or even bad, as long as they didn't notice I was dumb.**

Not only were my needs never addressed, but any inclinations or talents were buried under all my problem areas. I also have a speech impediment, a lisp, that could have been corrected fairly easily if I had consistent therapy as a child. I wonder how different my life would be if my childhood educational needs had been met.

I know I wasn't easy to teach. I was every teacher's worst nightmare. No amount of sticker or eraser bribing was successful. I was often punished by not being allowed out for recess or P.E., which is just about the worst thing you can do for an active boy.

I remember one particular teacher who really had it out for me. Ms. H. made it clear she didn't like me and thought I was a lost cause. Students could earn Friday afternoon free time for good behavior. Most of the class would earn free time every Friday, but I never could. Every Friday morning, I would start the day determined to be good, but I had no self-control or focus and would end up sulking in the classroom with Ms. H. while everyone else was free. I felt like there was no way to win with her, and she was happy about punishing me.

Another year, I had a hippie teacher who tried to do a relaxation exercise with the class. We sat with our hands folded and our eyes closed, picturing a calm place. Just as a hush fell over the room, I let out a long, loud fart. Everyone burst into laughter, and the class Ms. Hippie had just quieted was completely carried away. I think I brought all of my teachers to tears at some point.

At the end of sixth grade, my report card said that I had passed and would be moving on to middle school. A wave of relief washed over me. I was so proud of myself until a kid ripped it out of my hand laughing. "You got all F's, stupid," he sneered as he waved the pink paper in the air for everyone to see. Sure enough, I had failed every single subject, but they passed me anyway. And they continued to pass me every year as I fell further and further behind.

I went to school for something to do, to eat lunch, and to see my friends. It was just a place to hang out and socialize. I wasn't learning. I was put in special education classes, punished, scolded, and sent to the principal's office, but no one took the time to actually sit down and teach me. Between bouncing around from house to house, being expelled, and going to Juvenile Hall, I went on to attend six different high schools in San Jose before I dropped out at seventeen. Schoolwork made me feel like a loser. I learned to find acceptance in other ways.

Chapter 4

Drama and Drug Raids

I just wanted to curl up and cry, but I stood frozen, petrified, and afraid to move after that.

When I was about five years old, Mom started dating my dad's cousin Ernest, an upper-level drug-lord. He looked and dressed like he was a stunt double for Al Pacino in *Carlito's Way* with a beard, creased slacks, and beatle boots. We left my grandma's house on the east side to move into his house in a nice neighborhood in south San Jose. He had a son, Little Ernest, who lived there with us as well. Little Ernest was about two years younger than me. It seemed to Roy and me that we got blamed for everything while Little Ernest got away with murder.

My new school was predominantly white. The kids at my new school were not like kids from my old neighborhood. They looked different, talked different, and their families were very different. It was a completely new world. I wanted to fit in, but the more I tried the more I was excluded. I was the bad Mexican kid. I was repeatedly sent to the principal's office, but at this school, the principal spanked me with a big wooden paddle with holes in it to make it more aerodynamic. I felt humiliated and labeled. Once, when I was in third grade, I knew I was being sent to the office for a whoopin', so I just walked home in the middle of the day crying. It was frustrating always being in trouble.

Mom and Ernest had a new baby when I was seven, my little brother Isaac. I didn't like Mom's new boyfriend, but I wanted him to like me. I ached for a real dad, one that was always around. Mom was beautiful, and now she was able to buy beautiful clothes, big fur coats, and suede boots. Roy and I had all the stuff we begged for, Hush Puppies shoes, KangaROOS sneakers, TI sweatsuits, and OP t-shirts.

I remember when they were first dating, and Ernest probably wanted to impress Mom, he took me and Roy to Great America amusement park. We went on "The Demon" roller coaster ride together, and he bought me an overpriced souvenir hat with the ride's logo. I couldn't believe he splurged on me like that. "He must really like me," I thought. Later I lost the hat and cried and cried. It wasn't because I liked the hat so much but because of what it meant to me. I wanted Earnest to know I appreciated it and took care of it. I didn't want him to think I carelessly lost it.

There were lots of parties at our house. Sometimes it was fun, but some nights Roy, Little Ernest, and I were locked in our bedrooms so the adults could party down. Our bedrooms were across the hall from each other. They would tie our doors together so we couldn't get out. We would yell to each other through the door trying to devise a plan, calling out directions, when to pull on the door in a joint effort. It never worked. We eventually gave up and fell asleep.

We had fun times too, but I knew we were always on shaky ground. In a moment, things could shift from big birthday parties and barbeques to fighting or one of Ernest's rages.

He even told Roy to cut off his arm in one of his drug-induced screaming fits. That was one of the scariest moments because Ernest was totally irrational, and I knew Roy hated Ernest and really wanted to do it. I could see Roy struggling with the decision as he held the knife in his hand and Ernest taunted him and screamed for him to do it. I can only imagine what kind of terrors plagued Ernest's mind while he was high. During many of his PCP (Angel Dust) episodes, he would hit my mom. As soon as he sobered up, he would sheepishly beg her to take him back, which she always did.

During one beating, Roy grabbed a meat cleaver and struck Ernest from behind as he was hitting Mom. Roy yelled at Mom to leave. "Go! Go! Just get out!" Mom grabbed my baby brother Isaac and ran out, leaving her eleven-year-old son to finish the fight. I was horrified. I didn't want to leave Roy there alone, but at eight years old, I was way too scared to stay. I quickly followed after Mom.

At his first chance, my brother bolted out the back door. Just as Ernest was about to catch him, Roy ran over the red lava rocks in the perfectly landscaped yard. Roy wasn't the fastest runner, being a little chubby, but he never wore shoes, so his feet were completely calloused. He picked up speed over the sharp rocks as Ernest was forced to come to a halt and carefully ease through on tender bare feet. Roy hopped the fence and jumped into the car Mom and I had idling on the street behind our house.

Ernest tried to beat me plenty of times too, but I was too fast for him. I always managed to disappear when I knew I had it coming.

One morning I awoke early to a loud crashing sound. Roy and I walked out the front door to see Mom smashing Ernest's beige Chevy Monte Carlo with a hammer. He loved cars and had two different T-Birds plus the Monte Carlo. Red, white, and yellow shards of glass spread across the driveway. Roy reached out a protective arm to keep me from walking any closer. We huddled together trembling. I saw a bloody gash above Mom's left cheekbone and a dark bruise already spreading across her swollen eye. A horrifying nausea rose up from my stomach to my head. I wanted to kill that coward Earnest. It was degrading to be a powerless little boy when my mother needed a strong man to protect her.

Ernest kept large stashes of cocaine and angel dust (PCP) around. Roy and I once even started playing on the roof with a cellophane-wrapped brick ounce, not knowing what it was.

There was a park across the street from our house where construction workers were building a new baseball diamond. Those construction workers were actually a surveillance team monitoring our home.

One summer morning I sat eating my Cap'n Crunch cereal and watching cartoons when a fully armed S.W.A.T. team busted through our front door. They made us all get down on the floor while some of them rushed through to get Ernest. They slammed Mom on the ground with full force and handcuffed her. Ernest managed to temporarily escape and run through the neighborhood in his tighty-whitey briefs until they tackled him. The police were there the entire day searching the house and questioning Ernest and Mom.

At one point, I started walking to get a toy that I had been playing with earlier. The officer spun around with his gun pointed right at me and shouted not to move. It was terrifying. I don't know what he thought I was trying to do. I was only about eight years old. It was scary to have cops yelling with guns blazing and my mom cuffed. **I just wanted to curl up and cry, but I stood frozen, petrified, and afraid to move after that.** They eventually let Mom go and arrested Ernest.

We had to move out immediately. The next day we packed up to go back to Grandma's. My dad came over to help. I was relieved Earnest was out of our lives and that I could have some peace back at Grandma's house.

I guess Dad knew his cousin was going to be locked up for a while. Dad never missed an opportunity to come up. He started packing up all of Ernest's snazzy clothes. I remember seeing him standing in the walk-in closet trying on all the "cool threads," which didn't really fit his style, especially the boots. Dad made me laugh, but it wasn't exactly funny how he had an uncanny sense of when to show up at times that were convenient for him, because he wasn't there when I really needed him.

Dad was right about Ernest not needing the clothes though. Ernest ended up doing some hard time and was out of our life for good. Sadly, he never even saw much of his own son, my brother Isaac.

Ernest passed away in 2012. I received the news that he had died when I was in Washington D.C. for the National Forum on Youth Violence Prevention. My dad, his cousin, seemed pretty saddened by the news. At his memorial service, I was relieved to hear that Ernest put his faith in Christ just before his death.

CHAPTER 5

Fighting to Find Myself

I had finally done something well.

When I was in sixth grade, I attended Lee Mathson Middle School, where I got into my first real fight. It was with a big kid named Tony. We were both in the same grade, but he seemed huge, and I felt like a puny elementary school kid compared to him.

My best option at first was to run. I left the schoolyard and ran up to the catwalk going over the freeway. I hoped I could just outrun Tony and get away without having to take a beating. I had seen some pretty crazy fights now that I was in junior high. One I could never forget, especially now, was when a Puerto Rican kid from Chicago beat up a seventh grader. He jumped onto his back and tore at him like he wanted to kill him. I saw him actually sink his teeth into his forehead and rip the skin off. It gave me a sick feeling

POST.
traumatic
QUEST

in my stomach, and I tried to go unnoticed by him for the rest of the year.

Things could get pretty rough, and I knew Tony could really hurt me, but that's not what made me scared. It was the humiliation, having to cower down and just wait until it was over, knowing it would just happen again. Being hurt and afraid was normal for me. My older brother and cousins were always picking on me.

It wasn't just your typical teasing either. They were ruthless: tying me up in the closet, locking me out of the house naked, pushing me in the deep end of the pool when I didn't know how to swim. They would punch me, kick me, and hit me, so I was now used to all that. I was shaking because I had never been in a real fight. Not like this, where everyone was watching. Girls and older kids were gathering round, and my big brother was there too. Roy didn't care how bad he hurt me, but I knew he didn't want anyone else beating me up. I was his little brother after all; we were a team.

Tony caught up to me and knocked me to the ground. I hit the back of my head hard and my face scraped into the cement of the bridge. Cars rushed by on the freeway below. The wind howled, whipping the girls' hair. Everyone stood around watching with smiles on their faces as the blood pounded in my head.

Suddenly, the air seemed to go silent. I somehow managed to spring up fast, and as I did, all the pain and fear just melted away. I was completely overpowered by a cold hard rage. The anger swallowed everything else up. Nothing could stop me now, and I wasn't afraid of anything. It felt good.

My fist hit him right on the cheekbone, connecting with a crack. I could tell he was stunned. I saw the water well up in his eyes with pain and shock. He wasn't expecting that. I felt my confidence explode, and I started swinging as fast as I could. Blow after blow, head, face, shoulder, stomach. Within a matter of seconds, he was on the ground crying, holding his stomach, rocking back and forth. I looked around, wondering if I should stop now. As I caught my breath, I saw the look on all the kid's faces—awe. They couldn't believe that little Danny took down big Tony, the kid that ruled the schoolyard.

I heard laughter and the boys screaming, "Yeah! Yeah!" in amazement. I stood proud, the winner. I looked over at Roy and saw him swell with pride. It's hard to express the feeling in words: empowerment, accomplishment. It was a new experience to go after something and master it. **I had finally done something well.** I was cool. Now people would like me, respect me, even be afraid of me. Who wants to take me on now? I thought. I can take on anyone.

It was a defining moment in my life. I knew who I was. I had found my identity in fighting.

Today I am a peacemaker. I break up fights and help students realize fighting doesn't solve anything. It perpetuates pain. I've even been inadvertently punched in the nose trying to stop a fight between a couple teenagers. I'm trained in mediation and conflict resolution. A great joy of my life is seeing two kids walk out shaking hands or hugging after resolving a disagreement. Most fights are over minor issues or some silly words. If I could have learned those skills as a child, perhaps the fighting wouldn't have dominated my life the way it did.

After that first fight, I never backed away from a confrontation. I was so daring not because I was brave, but because part of me wanted to die. Sometimes I got scared, but always I pushed it down until I felt that familiar numbness. Then I waited for the rage to rise up and take over. It became a comfort to me.

I wasn't the biggest, but I was the craziest. I didn't waste any time with trash talk or intimidation tactics. I would immediately rush anyone who I felt disrespected me. In high school, I knew my friends just used me because if anyone started messing with them, they knew I would take care of it. I think it was a form of entertainment for them. They didn't really care what happened to me, and honestly, neither did I.

I got back at the users in my own way. Yeah, we were friends, but they were scared of me. I could do whatever I wanted and treat them however I wanted, intimidating them to do things for me or give me things just like I used to cry to get my way when I was little. Pretty soon everyone was scared of me, just like I used to be scared.

CHAPTER 6

Nightmares and Visits to the Witch Doctor

My body seemed to remember the trauma before my conscious mind could.

I was afflicted with horrible night terrors most of my childhood and adolescence. I would awake in a cold sweat, up on my feet, screaming at the top of my lungs. My parents never consulted a doctor or got me any kind of formal treatment. That thought never seemed to cross anyone's mind; on the contrary, it seemed to be a joke to them. I always felt the need to protect my neck, and I couldn't fall asleep unless I covered it. I was also claustrophobic and absolutely terrified of the dark or sleeping in a room alone, embarrassingly even as a teenager. Roy knew my fears and thought they were hilarious, so he would lock me in a dark closet while I screamed and beat on the door. I remember waking up confused to Roy and his friend who had slept over, laughing at me. It even happened when I stayed at Camp MayMac.

Camp MayMac was a camp for underprivileged kids from East San Jose, located near Santa Cruz, California. I woke up standing in the middle of the cabin, all eyes staring at me with great concern. I honestly don't know what I dreamed or why. Now I understand this was a symptom of PTSD. Even as an adult, I would have a feeling of being strangled and wake up choking. I knew something bad had happened. Brief flashes of memory would bubble up with the physical sensation, but I would quickly push it away. Much later in life, through therapy, I remembered the terrifying incident of abuse. I believe it happened when I was a very young child.

I know there has been a battle for my soul all of my life. To cure me of my nightmares, Dad drove me out to a ranch to see a curandera (healer), who dunked me in a creek as if I were being baptized and ripped a pigeon apart over my head to get the "bad spirit" to leave me alone. It didn't help. My night terrors persisted. When I started drinking and using drugs, they were a lot less frequent. But using drugs brought on hallucinations that I was awake for, which was truly scary. They seemed incredibly real, and I believe there were a lot of dark spiritual things taking place.

In my life today, my wife and I love to go on hikes. We get the kids out of the house for long walks together as a family. On one of these occasions, we went to Alum Rock Park. I hadn't been there in years. My wife and I held swinging hands as our two little ones bounced around with all their kid energy and darted ahead of us on the trail. I called for them to stop and be careful not to fall. "Stay away from the edge!" I yelled. I didn't want them falling off as we continued up the incline. My warnings became more and more panicked. My wife told me to relax. "They're not doing anything wrong. They're just being kids. They're just walking." The trail was actually pretty wide.

I couldn't shake the mounting alarm, and I continued to snap at them if they stepped out of arm's length. We came to the top of the hill and looked out at the beautiful vista. We peered down over the valley below us and pointed to different landmarks we could make out in the distance. We walked around taking in the different views, but I couldn't shake the uneasy feeling. My heart was pounding. I found myself standing in the shadow of Eagle Rock, a huge rock at the top of the hill. It's not a rock you can walk up; you would have to climb up on your hands and knees. It is considerably steep, and there is not a flat space at the top. The entire rock is uneven and jagged.

Suddenly a vivid memory came to me clearly. I remembered being there as a young boy with my dad. Dad was drunk and laughing. He was swinging me by my arms at the top of Eagle Rock. He swung me around in a circle and my little body flailed out over the canyon. He spun me in the air again and again. I realized now how reckless and terrifying this was. It's a wonder Dad didn't lose his footing, flinging me off the cliff to my death. This was why I kept feeling an overpowering fear of my kids falling and why I was experiencing so much anxiety. **My body seemed to remember the trauma before my conscious mind could.**

I was frequently in harmful, scary, or abusive situations. I never thought too much about it when things like that would happen. It seemed normal to me, and I just learned to deal with the stress. In the moment, I acted like nothing happened and survived, but the fear and trauma would pop up at other times, in other ways.

I grew up going to Alum Rock and Hellyer Park, or various friends' ranches. The adults would barbeque, drink, and smoke. The kids would run around for hours unsupervised. We did the same thing at home. I was a very young child out alone for hours, running the streets, filthy, sweaty, getting into all kinds of trouble. The other neighborhood kids did the same. We ran around until all the kids eventually got cold or hungry enough to go home.

When my two youngest kids were born, I often felt anxious about their safety. As they grew, I watched over them like a hawk at every moment when playing at the park or anytime we were outside. I felt uneasy if they were out of immediate reach or if they momentarily escaped my eyesight. I can't believe I used to run the streets all day long at their age. Anything could have happened to me. Plenty of things did happen.

Jonah and Michal-Donna on one of our family hikes

CHAPTER 7

Death and Dying for a Dad

Jealousy would wash over me as I looked on as an outsider, feeling alone.

I was aware of death from a young age. One of my earliest memories is just a quick flash of my uncle Bobby playfully throwing me in the air. I must have been very young, because he died in a swimming accident when I was two and he was only fifteen. He was my dad's youngest brother. His loss was a big part of my family.

Dad, my uncles, me, and my Grandpa

There was loss on my mom's side of the family as well. On Friday nights, we would beg to go to my Uncle Victor's. His two boys were about the same age as Roy and me. My cousins were like brothers to us. We loved hanging out together. I liked being around my Uncle Victor too, so I always wanted to be there.

Victor's brother, my Uncle Charlie, had been killed in Vietnam. I remember seeing Uncle Victor late at night with a bottle of booze in his hands, sobbing his heart out over his brother with the music blasting. He would be singing along with tears running down his cheeks. My Uncle Charlie was missed and remembered. Maybe I would die young someday too, and everyone would miss me.

My paternal grandmother Pura died when I was fourteen. It was a completely devastating loss to me, although I couldn't really process it. And when I was about fifteen, my maternal Grandma Julia became debilitated for the rest of her life. I remember hearing my mother finding her in bed one morning. "Mom! Mom!" Her voice rose each time as she repeated it over and over with no response. Grandma had had a stroke.

She needed full-time care as she was completely immobile on her right side and had lost the ability to speak. She had been the rock of our family, had given me a sense of security. She held everything together and took care of all of us with her hot meals and warm home. Her home was my home, and I knew that no matter what happened I could go back to Grandma's house and she would take me in and care for me. Now that had all changed.

My grandfather refused outside assistance. He said that his wife had cared for him all of his life; now he wanted to personally take care of her, and he did. Everyone was surprised to see a new side to him through his unselfish behavior and devotion to her.

Even though she could no longer speak because of the stroke, Grandma Julia would clasp her hands together when she saw me to let me know she was praying for me. I understood what she was communicating as I leaned down to kiss her cheek. She would reach up to hold my face close to hers a moment longer. Even though she couldn't speak, I knew she was saying, "Love you mijo. Be good." She never stopped praying for me no matter how bad I was.

Grandma Julia and me after her stroke

Grandma Julia with me and my cousins

Who would have thought that years later her prayers would be answered and so much more? What the Lord has done in my life has far surpassed all my hopes and dreams, and I'm sure it exceeded Grandma's prayers as well. The love of grandparents, or just one person, can make a huge difference in someone's life.

———

When I was about eleven, my father left his second wife and the daughter he had with her, my sister Angie. Shockingly, he started dating a teenage girl who became his third wife. She is four years older than my brother Roy. After I became an adult, my dad sometimes had girlfriends that were younger than I was. He went on to have three more children with his third wife before they divorced: Jessica, Ely, and Travis. They married while she was still a minor to protect my dad from criminal charges because she was pregnant.

I saw my dad being affectionate with the younger kids, his new family. **Jealousy would wash over me as I looked on as an outsider, feeling alone.** "I wish I had what they had," I thought. They had a real family and dad in their home. Dad must have sensed this because during different seasons in life, even to this day, he would give me gifts or shove cash in my hand. "Just take it, mijo." I could tell he felt guilty about not being there for me in the way I needed when I was growing up. He wanted to make it up to me, but he continued on in his destructive ways.

Dad was often out front in the driveway for hours working on cars. He had cherry cars, and he worked on other people's rides as well. Beautiful classic cars would be parked down our street. He let me help him sand the cars to prep for painting. He showed me how to sand off the paint using a crisscross motion. Learning his tricks and techniques made me feel important. I felt so proud whenever I got to drive around with him in one of his bombs or his '59 Chevy El Camino.

Whatever my dad did, I idolized. The fact that he was crooked didn't stop my need to emulate and look up to him, just like all young boys want a father they can respect. When he was selling drugs, I imagined him to be the most powerful drug dealer. When I went to visit him in jail, I thought he was the baddest dude there. When I was a child, he could do no wrong in my eyes. I craved his attention and affection. I didn't understand that he had his own problems to work through.

When I was in middle school, my new young stepmom took us to visit Dad in prison a few times. We got to stay overnight with Dad in a home for family visitors. It was great seeing my dad again and getting to actually spend time with him. Even though we were on the correctional facility premises, to me, it was like being on vacation. I was disappointed because the correctional officers wouldn't let me bring in my handheld Nintendo, but I was excited to stay in this big house with my dad. Dad had a new hairstyle, a duck tail. His hair was shaved close all over except for a long piece in the back that was braided and hung down the back of his neck. I asked him if he could cut my hair in the same style. My stepmom snickered at me. "How do you think he's gonna cut your hair? He's in prison." Everything in the dorm we were staying in was carefully monitored down to the smallest detail, and razors weren't allowed.

As an adult looking back, I can see how sad it was. The whole time we were there helicopters were bringing in massive loads of seized marijuana. The helicopters blared through, dumping the plants where they would be set ablaze in huge bonfires.

Little did I know that I would be returning there, not as a visitor but as a prisoner.

CHAPTER 8

Strong Armed Robbery and Stays in Juvie

I tried my best to act "normal" on the outside, but I sure didn't feel normal.

When I was a freshman in high school, I had a friend named Sam who was eighteen and into criminal pursuits. He had started purse snatching. My other friend Jesse took his mom's van, and we went cruising around. Sam stole some lady's purse off of her and ran around the corner to where we were waiting in the van, and we sped away.

We went back to Jesse's house and were taking some bottles out to be recycled when San Jose PD rolled up. Someone had written down the license plate number, and they tracked us down to Jesse's. They told us to freeze as they shined their spotlight on us.

Before I even knew he was missing, Sam had run through the backyard with lightning speed and jumped the fence. The lady, whose purse was stolen, was there. She got out and identified *me*! Before I knew what was happening, I was the one getting arrested! They booked Jesse and me and took me straight to Juvenile Hall that night, since I was being charged with strong armed robbery, a violent crime. It was common practice to detain youth before trial or sentencing. There has been significant reform in recent years, but this practice is still surprisingly common. I served thirty days at age fourteen.

My head was spinning from how fast everything happened. When they put me in that dark, tiny little cell, all my worst fears and nightmares came to life. I screamed and pleaded desperately. "Please don't make me sleep in here. Please, please, put me outside. Put me anywhere, just not in here. I can't breathe! I can't breathe!" I shrieked.

On top of everything else, it was freezing. Every night I was there I would shiver under my one thin flannel blanket. The air was filled with yelling, cussing, and piercing screams from heads peeping out of the box windows of cell doors.

I made it through that first horrible night. Once I spent a day or two taking notice of how things worked around there, I got pretty good at it. After being incarcerated, some people are full of remorse, vowing to change their ways and never go back again. Not me. The experience really hardened me.

I was shook from the shock and trauma of being locked up. **I tried my best to act "normal" on the outside, but I sure didn't feel normal.** I was surprised to see that my act was convincing because no one seemed to notice. I came out changed, but everyone else back home went on with their lives as if nothing had happened.

It was right at this time, when I was trying desperately to survive and put Juvenile Hall behind me, that my Grandma Pura had a horrible accident. A few days after I was released from my first stay, Grandma Pura slipped in the bathtub and hit her head so hard she fell into a coma. My aunts told me I needed to visit her in the hospital, but I couldn't handle it. "I'll go visit her tomorrow," I said a few times. I never got around to it, and soon after she died.

My Grandma Pura (my Dad's mom) was someone who loved me unconditionally. Most of my life I felt alone, but I knew I mattered to her. I would come to her house drunk and hungry at four in the morning, and she would open the door for me and feed me. Often, she would sleep out on the couch, waiting and praying for me.

She never made me feel bad for waking her late at night. In fact, I knew she was glad to have me safe in her home where she could watch over me. When I stumbled in late at night, I would sleep on the other couch, and she would stay with me on hers, making sure I was okay. We would fall asleep facing each other.

Grandma wore colorful muumuu dresses and would get her hair done in a bouffant style. She had light skin and dark hair. She was very pretty in her day. She and my Grandpa Joe were a beautiful couple. All the grandkids could grab candy money or money for the ice cream man from the big jar of pocket change she kept in the kitchen. She would laugh at my spiky hair and call me spider. She was always patient with me and never angry.

Grandma Pura Sanchez

I had just got out of Juvie and now my grandma was dead. I couldn't believe it. What was happening to my world? I felt awful that I hadn't visited her. I'm sure she made each one of her many grandchildren feel special, but all her love and attention made me feel like I was her favorite. She was the only person in my life who made me feel that way, and when she died, I truly felt her loss, the loss of her love. Sometimes when I was drunk or high, I would search for her grave at Oakhill Cemetery. That was the only way I could face her memory through my guilt.

I would return to Juvenile Hall every year until I was eighteen, when I moved on to jail and then prison. Just as some people study their craft and move up the ladder in their career field, so I became almost like an animal to stay on top in this system. I was a psycho, throwing chairs at people, slamming them with cafeteria trays, and taking everything as a challenge.

In 1989, I was sixteen and once again in Juvie. I had been placed in solitary confinement as punishment for fighting. One day I was in my cell all alone when everything started shaking. The shaking and shifting kept getting stronger and seemed to last forever, but in reality, it was only a matter of seconds. I could hear all the other boys around me freaking out, but I couldn't see them. I was all alone in that cell. And I was far away from my family.

It was the Loma Prieta Quake of '89. It was terrifying. I knew it was every man for himself in there. At that time, all the doors in Juvenile Hall had manual locks. In order to be let out, a guard would have to come around and unlock each door individually. There was obviously nothing to break in there, but I was panicked with the fear of being buried alive under the walls of cement. This anxiety would come over me during each aftershock for days afterward.

Every time I was incarcerated after that, those thoughts were there. I would always wonder what would happen if there were some kind of natural disaster. It was a huge fear of mine because I felt that our lives weren't valued as inmates, so rescuing us would not be a priority.

Years later, one of the most devastating days in our generation's history would take place while I was incarcerated.

CHAPTER 9

Running From The Ranch, The Boys Ranch

Being constantly worried about being caught and sent back added to my base level of stress and anxiety.

A majority of justice-involved youth have experienced significant trauma in their lifetime. Today there is thankfully a call for trauma-informed care. I hope to see more efforts being made in that direction. I believe reducing juvenile incarceration and reforming the model will lead to a reduction in adult incarceration.

I went in and out of various types of detention facilities throughout my teen years. I had no boundaries at home. Mom was busy, and I didn't listen anyway. The only structure I knew was being incarcerated. Since I didn't have a healthy or supportive structure at home, incarceration gave me the sense of order and safety I needed. It gave me routine, three square meals a day, scheduled sleeping, eating and shower times, and strict discipline.

But I had no self-discipline, no skills to self-monitor my own behavior. As soon as I got out, I would celebrate by being even more destructive and dangerous.

My first escape from one of these facilities gave me a newfound thrill. I was locked up at a coed facility called the Wright Center. It has since closed, but it was located out in the boondocks near Calero Park hills in south San Jose.

The Wright Center had different levels or belts based on behavior. You could earn an 8-hour pass, 24-hour pass, or 72-hour weekend pass for good behavior. One Friday night, while everyone else got to go home, I had been demoted for getting in trouble. My friend also had to stay behind, and we were working in the kitchen together, pissed that we couldn't leave. So, we hatched a plan to escape. Since most people were gone for the weekend, we were able to hop the fence and run down the hill undetected.

We ran through the dark woods and felt like wartime soldiers trying to sneak past our enemies or like we had just escaped a chain gang. To me it seemed like there was an all-points bulletin out for us and every type of law enforcement officer had been activated for our immediate capture. I swear I could hear helicopters circling above the eerily tall eucalyptus trees. I was ready for cops around every corner, jumping out with guns.

In reality, they weren't that concerned because I wasn't taken back until I was arrested again for another crime. **Being constantly worried about being caught and sent back added to my base level of stress and anxiety.** I was in a recurring state of alarm.

When I was sent back, I ended up escaping a few more times. Once by hiding in a creek and getting stuck in the mud, where the "A" boys, the best-behaved kids, found me and dragged me back kicking. They used to send the "A" kids out to look for anyone that ran. I assume this practice is no longer legal.

Over ten years ago, I was invited to speak to the youth at the Wright Center. One of the staff there remembered me. He spoke to me warmly and was delighted to see my transformation. The center has since closed. Some of the other centers I was confined at have closed or have been changed to more residential style programs.

Unfortunately, there have not been as many changes to the adult incarceration system I grew up to become a part of.

CHAPTER 10

Jumped in and Doin' Drive Bys

"He who does not love does not know God, for God is love."

I John 4:8

We never talked too much about that pain, but we all knew we shared it.

Besides fighting, I never really had anything I was good at. I never played organized sports. My parents never drove me to practice or cheered me on from the bleachers. My dad didn't practice with me in the front yard and teach me the insides of the game like I saw other dads do. There were no little league photos, snazzy sports uniforms, applause from the stands, trophies, or strait-laced little teammate buddies going out for pizza after the game. But when I was in seventh grade, I fell in love with skateboarding.

Roy's friend gave me his used JFA board. The board was old and falling apart, but I loved it so much. The first time I ever skateboarded, I hopped on and immediately knew how to ride. I was a natural. I felt like I had finally found my niche.

At that time, I knew only a few other people that skated in my circle. Skating became everything to me. I went to Alva skate jams, hung out at Go Skate skate shop next to the Almaden Twin movie theater, and skated day and night. I would be scraped up, dirty and sweaty, skating hours and hours on end. It was an escape for me, my own world. I learned quickly how to ollie and do tricks.

As time went on, I met other skaters. It was a diverse community. I listened to heavy metal, and I also looked different from everyone else. I was *Suicidal Tendencies* meets cholo skate punk. I wore flannels with baggy Bens and a bleached blond Steve Caballero haircut.

Over the years people would often start stuff with me because of my looks. They thought I was just some rocker or punk skateboarder who wouldn't do anything. They didn't know I was ready to rumble if I perceived anything as even the slightest insult. I would hit people with my skateboard or throw something at them. When they were distracted trying to catch it, I would start pounding on them.

Some of my friends were small-time hood drug dealers. We used to put PCP-laced joints in cassette tape holders and walk around selling them for twenty bucks. After the movie Colors came out, I felt like the climate in San Jose changed. Everyone wanted to bang, and all the wannabes wanted to prove they were hard. I was really just a wannabe, but even I had the potential for murder. That's the scary thing about teens with no boundaries, longing to be accepted.

They have no concept of the seriousness and far-reaching impact of their rash decisions.

At about sixteen years old, I was jumped into a local gang. It was a newly established gang, an old hood with a new name. We were a small, tight-knit crew. Being a part of the gang gave me a false sense of security, a feeling of camaraderie and family. Even taking the physical blows while being jumped in made me feel loved and accepted like I never had before. I think we all really came together because of our pain. **We never talked too much about that pain, but we all knew we shared it.** It was pretty obvious we were all messed up. Many of them had been locked up too and had dads that had been in and out of prison like mine. I know some of those friends were dealing with serious loss. I had lost my grandma, but they had lost parents or siblings in horrible ways.

They didn't mind my weird style. They accepted me like I was. I wanted to prove to them that I was worth it. I was willing to do anything to show them. At age sixteen, there was a moment when everything could have changed. But God's merciful hand protected me from myself.

Friends from the local gang I was in had already been doing drive-bys and taking shots at rival gang members. On a weekend night, we cruised into the nightclub parking lot where all our rivals stood smoking out by their cars. I wasn't looking for a particular person, just an easy shot. I had a reputation of being a brutal fighter, but I wanted to do something really crazy. I wanted to take it to the next level and solidify my reputation by shooting someone.

I saw one loner walking away from the crowd. I was in the passenger seat with a sawed-off shotgun in my right hand, ready to lean out the window. I slowly eased my hand up, keeping the gun just below the window so it couldn't be seen. He looked up and I locked eyes with my target. I saw recognition in his eyes, and it was obvious that we both knew exactly what was about to go down.

But a split second before I was about to shoot, a cop drove by, right in between us. I carefully shoved the gun back under the seat. The driver played it cool but drove home in a hurry.

Today I am haunted by the far-reaching pain this type of senseless violence causes. My mind flashes with images of the things I've seen in my work as a Community Chaplain—the pain of a single father losing his only son, the desperate cry of a mother whose son was brutally murdered in cold blood, pregnant girlfriends wrapping their arms around coffins, refusing to let go, little brothers with fear in their eyes when they see how death approaches without warning. This pain wears on me and breaks my heart. I can't believe at one time I was so desensitized that I took part in this lifestyle.

That night, so long ago it is like another lifetime, we thought we were lucky we didn't get pulled over. Now I know just how fortunate I really was. The driver of the car that night was a close friend of mine who is now serving life in prison for murder. The three other passengers are also serving a life sentence for the same crime.

Thankfully, this was one of the only times I can remember having access to a gun or who knows where I would be. It pains me to see so many young kids who have access to guns today without understanding they are playing with fire that will spread out of control and burn everything in its path.

CHAPTER 11

Sex, Drugs, and Rock n' Roll

I went on to self-medicate through drugs and alcohol for many years, which led to more bad choices, multiplying the pain and suffering in my life.

I started having sex and using drugs and alcohol at a young age, all around twelve or thirteen. That's what happens when you're left to roam around at all hours. At first, I didn't want to drink because I didn't want to end up like my dad. My thoughts changed after the first time I really got drunk. All the pain and fear melted away in a warm comfort. I felt like I was enjoying life for the first time, but in reality, it was only temporarily numbing the pain of the trauma and emptiness I couldn't cope with.

We walked around the corner of Story and King Road where everyone was out cruising and ended up at a park. My brother remembers that night well. I don't remember much because I was passed out on a merry-go-round at the park. Roy and my cousins spun it faster and faster as my limp body dangled from the big bars of the old metal merry-go-round. They left and came back to find me still spinning, but very slowly now with a loud creaking sound on each turn. One of my arms limply hung off the side. My fingers dangled, raking lines in the sand. They couldn't stop laughing. I was really out cold. When I came to, I refused to go home. I wanted to stay out, keep drinking, and have some more "fun."

I quickly progressed to all types of drugs. Sadly, I have tried just about every type of drug that was available during the 1990s, with the exception of heroin and IV drugs. It was exciting, and I looked forward to the pleasure of it at first, but there was nothing pleasurable about the outcome. Once I was in a PCP-induced hallucination tirade so bad that my brother had to tie me up outside with a telephone cord. I thought there were ants crawling all over me. Over the years there were nights I would fly into angry rants directed at God, blaming Him for my problems and screaming at Him to leave me alone.

I went on to self-medicate through drugs and alcohol for many years, which led to more bad choices, multiplying the pain and suffering in my life. The only limit to my alcohol consumption was how much I could afford to buy or manage to steal. Sometimes I consumed entire bottles of hard liquor. My addiction was so severe that I would be physically ill if I didn't drink. Beer runs were part of my normal routine. I would walk into a grocery store, fill up a cart to overflowing with all kinds of alcoholic beverages, and just walk right out the automatic doors in broad daylight. This worked for me a number of times. These were the days before the sticker sensors. Alcohol led me to dig a deeper and deeper pit for myself that I couldn't get out of.

Chapter 12

Shackled by Shame

No matter how much I tried to forget the abuse, it still tortured me.

By age 15, I was already a heavy drinker. After Grandma Pura passed away and Grandma Julia had her stroke, I felt like I was drifting without those anchors in my life. I had the eerie sense of reckless freedom because I didn't have to think about letting down my grandma or making her worry now that she was gone. I was struck with the cold emptiness of my grandmother's absence and care.

There were house parties just about every weekend with various friends. I usually ended up getting drunk out of my mind. One night, I got stranded far from home. I decided to hoof it back. Soon it started raining. I was drunk, exhausted, freezing, and soaked to the bone. Some guy pulled over and offered me a ride, which I gladly accepted, happy to be out of the rain. The real reason he stopped was not to give me a ride but to take something from me. I was sexually abused.

It cloaked me in a dark cloud of shame that I was unable to escape no matter how hard I tried. I felt stupid and guilty. I thought being sexually assaulted was something that happened to innocent little kids, not a teenager like me. I didn't even realize what had happened was abuse from an adult to a child until many years later. I didn't think of it in those terms. I thought there must have been something wrong with me, and it led to the most horrible and sickening feelings. I tried to pretend that it never happened. **But no matter how much I tried to forget the abuse, it still tortured me.** I would drink and get high to block out the feeling.

I thought I was the only one who went through this, but now I know many men are dealing with the same thing. There are many myths and false narratives around male sexual abuse, and it goes highly unreported.

When my brother Roy was eighteen and I was fifteen, he found out that my dad was not his biological father. If you recall, my parents had a shotgun wedding when my mom was six months pregnant with Roy, and he was named a junior after my father. When my parents split up six years later, my dad and his sisters figured out the dates and realized that he couldn't be the father. He asked my mom and she admitted it. They kept the secret all of Roy's childhood.

On Roy's eighteenth birthday, Mom told him the truth. Roy was completely caught off guard. He had never suspected. He went out, got wasted, and came home so upset he punched me. When I fell on the floor, he kicked me in the face. He said he was mad that I had a dad and he didn't.

All of our lives Dad had been careful to treat Roy just like his own son; a little too careful, because it seemed to me like he loved Roy more. To this day, they are very close. I always felt like both of my parents favored Roy, maybe out of guilt, so I didn't really see what the big deal was. I didn't have the capacity to empathize or see beyond my own needs and feelings.

Through the years, I physically fought with several of Mom's boyfriends. I hated having different men sleeping in my home and acting like they owned the place. When I was a small boy, I would just run from them, tucking and rolling out of windows to escape. When I got older, I didn't run, I attacked. When I was a teenager, my friends and I would take Mom's car, party at her house when she wasn't home, and take money out of her purse. You can see why she and her boyfriends were mad. Often, I would come home drunk after the bars closed, telling Mom to get up to make me something to eat, waking the whole house. My brothers would defend my mom, and I would play the victim, like I was ganged up against.

I expected family members to drop everything and meet every request I made, whether it was a request for money or a knock in the middle of the night asking to sleep over; but I had no ability to be there for them in return. Luckily, I had a lot of friends so my couch surfing circuit could last over a month without going to the same place twice.

When my mom sent me to live with family members a few times during my teen years, I felt discarded. I was convinced that meant she had given up on me and I was beyond hope. It was kind of family members to take me in, but I couldn't see it that way. I believed I was a burden to everyone. I had no home or anywhere I was truly wanted. I had an underlying feeling of abandonment and insecurity that shaped the way I interacted with the world.

I was so insecure that I would blow up if my mom spent one penny more on my brothers than she did on me. She would take us back-to-school shopping and I would constantly be suspicious she was buying my brothers more than me because she loved them more. The more abandoned I felt by my mom, a girlfriend, or a loved one, the more I would turn into a monster, growling outrageous orders that in my mind I set up as a test of their love for me. If they refused to meet my demands, I would flip out and accuse them of betrayal. The impression that I was unlovable increased my reckless behavior. It was a dangerous pattern that would destroy virtually every relationship in my life.

The same things that help you survive incarceration are the very things that prevent you from being close to people in the free world. You become good at tuning out and shutting down. Never trusting anyone, greediness, the mind games and fronts, they're all programmed into your thinking so you don't even realize how sick you are.

I became a father at age seventeen when my son Daniel was born. I have a picture of me holding my precious firstborn right after his birth. I am just a skinny child myself with a big smile and a black eye from a fight the night before. He was an adorable, tiny baby, less than six pounds. I was terrified of dropping him because he was so small. I would hold him close to my chest, trying to be as gentle and careful as possible.

My son Daniel and me

I wanted to be a good dad, but I had absolutely no concept of what that meant, so nothing changed.

I already told you that when I was twenty-four, I was stabbed and sent to jail, where I tried and hated Christianity. My daughter Minna was born while I was inside. I met her for the first time when she was four months old and fell in love with my sweet little girl. I was at one of my lowest points, and she brought new life and gave me a reason to live.

When I got out, I moved in with my kids and their mom. Most nights I ended up sleeping on the couch out in the living room. Minna would crawl and then eventually toddle over to me early in the morning while it was still dark. I would pull her up on the couch to snuggle with me. She was actually the one comforting me though. Her cuddles melted my heart. Her unconditional love was what I needed. She didn't know how bad I was; she just loved me as her daddy.

I adored both my kids so much. But at the same time, I was struggling. Some of the lyrics I wrote for my band at the time show my desperation:

> *Oh God, can you help me?*
> *I feel so damned confused.*
> *Oh God, come and save me.*
> *I feel washed up and abused.*

I wanted to be in a loving relationship, but I didn't have that modeled in my life. I knew sleeping with a girl often led to an instant relationship, so I did that a lot. I was chasing a deep connection, but after a while that connection usually faded and ended with the girl hating me for what a jerk I was. Sadly, even at that point, I could usually get them to take me back if I really tried. It made me feel in control when I had women that would do whatever I wanted, from car rides in the middle of the night for me and my friends to giving me money or buying me things. I liked it when a girl was desperate for me and would stay with me no matter what. I had burned all my bridges and didn't have anyone in my life I felt really loved me—I believed my parents and family had given up on me long ago—so I tried to find that unconditional love in romantic relationships. I wanted to see someone prove they loved me no matter what I did.

Carrying on a couple relationships at once made me feel secure too. I was terrified of being alone. If one of them didn't work out, I still had someone else. Ironically, the fact that I might have been cheating on them made the girls hold on to me a little tighter. Even the times I was caught, neither girl actually broke up with me. It seemed like each of them wanted to "win" by keeping me.

One day I was leaning back in the passenger seat of my girl-friend Yvette's car at a stoplight when my baby momma happened to pull up next to us. I looked over and was shocked to see her glaring at me. I was seeing both of them at the time, so I wasn't sure what I should do. I opened the door and got out and got into the car with my old lady and my toddler son. She was my kid's mom after all. "What are you doing?" Yvette yelled.

Once I was in the other car, the fighting started. Of course, she was furious, and after a few minutes I realized I didn't want to hear it and I didn't have to. I got out of the car and walked over to Yvette's friend's house, at the corner right by the stoplight we had just been at. Yvette was mad too, but what could she do? She didn't want me going back to my baby momma. It was a sick situation.

Yvette and I broke up after a few years, and I started dating her best friend Carina. Carina and I had a relationship that lasted several years as well. When my baby mama was eight months pregnant, she decided to confront my side chick at the time, Jen. Jen was the one she found out about, but I was seeing someone else as well, for a total of three steady girlfriends. Anyway, Jen didn't want the drama of an angry, pregnant girlfriend coming to her house, so our relationship fizzled out soon after. I wasn't too disappointed because I still had the two other women—Carina and my kids' mom. I didn't have to lose much sleep over the break-up.

While it was pleasurable, fun, and exciting, sex was also tinged with shame. I understand now that as a child, I experienced what is considered covert abuse. I had been oversexualized since my early childhood. Seeing, hearing, and being exposed to sexual situations at a young age is abusive in itself, whether or not there is physical assault. I didn't know that or know how to process the things I was exposed to. It just made me feel gross. Sex was something I needed, and it was a way to fill the connection that I craved, but at the same time it seemed like it had been ruined for me in some way.

After my life was changed through my faith, I went through a time of healing. Over the years my understanding of love and intimacy has grown and deepened. I feel great remorse for the way I treated people in the past and sad that way of life was common in my world.

CHAPTER 13

Suicidal Tendencies

Because of the way I had been abused sexually, I felt like I was always hiding a dark secret and pain that needed to come out.

For a long time, I was fascinated with the idea of suicide. A casual friend of mine hung himself when I was nineteen. When that happened, I couldn't get the suicidal thoughts out of my head. I had thought about it before, but now the intrusive thoughts constantly tormented me. I romanticized the idea and fantasized about my funeral and how all my loved ones would feel once I was gone. I would cut myself, burn myself, take too many pills, and wrap phone cords around my neck to see what it felt like. I hung a noose in my friend's garage, but I didn't go through with it. When he found it, he cried.

Because of the way I had been abused sexually, I felt like I was always hiding a dark secret and pain that needed to come

out. Once, during a bad fight with a girlfriend, I slashed my wrist with a kitchen knife. The police were called, and I was taken to the psych ward at Valley Medical Hospital on a seventy-two-hour hold. I guess they knew I wasn't too serious because I was released within hours.

But I still struggled as I watched other people grow up and find their way in life while I had nothing. And as bad as things were, I knew they would only get worse. I stayed with family, girlfriends, or friends, but I knew eventually every last person would tire of me and I would end up homeless. I didn't think change was possible. I was too far gone. My life continued to waste away. Instead of working to get out of the hole I was in and make a way for myself, I just drifted along into darker and darker stages, staying drunk or high most of the time. I lived a humiliating existence trying to believe I was cool.

Many people that seem to have their lives together are really just as broken and empty as I was. My life was so empty when it was just about me and what I wanted. Now that I am living for a higher purpose, my heart breaks for people who are stuck in an empty depression, perhaps putting on a happy face. Some of the same friends I used to look up to as having it all together are now calling me. They had material things, but without purpose, they were unsatisfied. I have talked with many people who admit that for years they were just fooling themselves.

Until my life was changed in 2003, suicide was an option that was always in the back of my mind. It comforted me in a strange way to know that if things didn't work out or got too bad, I could always kill myself as a way out. I had no idea that change was as simple as changing my mindset. But that wouldn't happen for many years.

CHAPTER 14

Fifty Man Brawl

I couldn't face how scary the whole situation actually was, so I made light of it.

It was five dollar per car night at The Capitol Drive-In Movies. People piled out of packed cars to hang out on lawn chairs with coolers of beer beneath silent movie screens. To get sound, there were big metal speakers you could turn on and attach to your car window. My friend Louie and I were drunk, acting stupid, and talking smack at the snack shack and arcade building in the middle of the drive-in. Louie decided to call it a night, and I was going to ride home with his cousin Robby, who was there with us. I started picking a fight with some dude, but four more of his friends came out and we all started going at it.

Pretty soon, people began gathering around to see the commotion and tons of his homies started joining in. He must have been rolling deep because before I knew it people were coming at me from every angle. The police report states that there were between thirty and fifty people involved. It was so bad that when the police eventually came on the scene, they couldn't break it up. It was totally out of control, a huge riot, except that everyone was against me.

My opponents got so mad because they couldn't get me down. Every time they attempted to knock me over, I would grab someone, leaning down on him, pushing myself up, and knocking him down in the process. I know this sounds unbelievable, but it was like an action movie. I was spinning around and ducking punches. I was always thinking at least three moves ahead during a fight. Even today, I love playing chess, and fighting is like chess on speed. I would scan my surroundings looking for opportunities, things I could use to my advantage. I completely shut off any pain and focused on my strategy. Adrenaline can cause your body to perform in amazing ways.

Remembering this scene, I see circles of people tightening in close and then letting up and expanding around me. A group would circle in attacking me. I was in the middle fighting with all my might and no reservations. I would manage to stay on my feet and fight them off. Then the circle would get bigger as they all backed away. Then the circle would form again as others closed in to try to stop me. Someone cracked my upper forehead and blood dripped off my eyebrows and down the middle of my nose. I must have looked like a rabid dog going buck wild with blood all over my face.

At one point, I grabbed someone and held him in front of me and his friends started socking him while trying to get at me. I thought Robbie was fighting with me, but apparently, he had managed to escape and pull up the car. As the car skidded up with a screech,

I dove in the window and tucked into the backseat. We sped off to Louie's house. I don't know how we managed to make it past the cops, but they were probably just glad to see us disperse at that point.

Louie lived in an old Victorian downtown that had very poor lighting at night. We walked up creaking stairs to the living room with thick, dark carpet. I felt shaky and high with adrenaline, and the first thing I wanted to do was get a drink. We had been rehashing the fight with Louie for a little while when his sister noticed I looked startlingly pale. Robby and Louie looked at me and agreed that I was as white as a ghost. We went to the kitchen to get some water. I was wearing black pants and a black sweatshirt. I felt all wet and sweaty and thought maybe I had fallen in some water. But in the light of the kitchen, we noticed I was bleeding. A puddle of blood had formed on the floor where I was standing. I had unknowingly been stabbed in my lower back.

Robby went to the store to get some rubbing alcohol and bandages. That's when he saw the backseat of his car was stained with blood. I waited in eerie calmness for him to come back and try to patch me up. The three of them were getting really freaked out as the blood continued to seep out of me, soaking the bandages instantly. Louie's sister decided to call 911. The dispatcher told her to have me wait outside. I casually laid down on the sidewalk, where my blood began to fan out onto the concrete. My mind was almost blank.

An ambulance and some police pulled up. The paramedics stepped out and cut off all my clothes and put me on a stretcher. It was full frontal nudity for all to see. All the while a detective was incessantly questioning me while the EMTs tried to stop the bleeding and find out where it was coming from. The detective was getting more aggressive. My friends started yelling at him, "Leave him alone already. He's f---ing dying!" Even the paramedics were upset and told him to back off.

They took me to the hospital where I was prepped for emergency surgery. The doctors ordered me to be rushed directly to the operating room, but there was one person ahead of me who had been shot. As soon as the OR was available, they wheeled me in for exploratory surgery to find out where I was bleeding. I was quietly lying on the operating table until I heard a metal tinkling and clashing from urgently moving hands. I slowly rolled my head around to see a tray full of tools and scalpels. That quickly snapped me out of my daze. I sprang up, screaming "You're not gonna cut me, are you? You're not gonna cut me!" A restraining arm pushed me back down and a clear mask was forced over my nose and mouth. The next thing I knew I woke up pleading, "Don't cut me! Don't cut me!" I thought it was the next second, but it was actually hours later in the recovery room.

I had been stabbed in the kidney. I have a huge scar in the middle of my stomach that runs all the way from my pubic bone to my breastbone, taking a sharp turn to go around my belly button. They sliced me wide open in a hurry to find out what was going on, removing and examining my organs. The surgeon found my kidney had been punctured and sewed up the wound. I was feeling all that pain now, a sharp pain deep in my abdomen and tenderness at even the slightest movement. I was kept in the hospital about two weeks. Because of this incident, the drive-in permanently discontinued the five-dollar car night.

You might wonder if I was scared and ready to change. I wasn't. **I couldn't face how scary the whole situation actually was, so I made light of it.** If someone would have had a serious heart-to-heart talk with me, I would have been forced to face the heaviness of what had really happened. I would have had to do some thinking about my choices and where they were leading me. Instead, I relished the attention. I had a lot of visitors in the hospital. Old friends I hadn't seen in a long time came by to stand in awe of my stab wounds and my brush with death. My friends thought I must have no fear in order to fight that many people. The truth was I just didn't have normal instincts to protect myself or care what happened to me.

The doctors strictly warned me not to drink after this. They listed all the dangers of consuming alcohol after my surgery, but I resumed my heavy drinking habit the week I got out. I was twenty-two.

CHAPTER 15

Gang Bangin' and Gettin' Down

They kicked me around and beat me while I contorted in pain, my hands and feet still tied behind my back.

Around the time I got in the fight at the drive-in, there were weeks on end where I was getting into fistfights every single day. Loving the attention, I frequently fought in front of clubs or bars with tons of people standing around watching. At those times, I was so pumped up I would take on two or three people at once with no problem, thinking I was hardcore.

I got in over my head plenty of times too. There were a few times I was knocked out cold. I've been choked out and have had numerous concussions. One time my friend A.V. and I got into a fight with a group of guys at Jack in the Box downtown after the bars closed. I was hit over the head with a chair from behind. When

I came to, I was outside on the ground with people standing around staring. I had a pounding headache, and I soon realized my wallet was missing. Aside from the pain, it was a really scary feeling being dominated like that, waking up disoriented.

To my great embarrassment, I was once knocked unconscious in front of a huge crowd. It was during the Sofa Street Fair Festival downtown, where crowds of people strolled along, and right in front of a jam-packed First Street Billiards with all eyes on me. I knew the dude was much bigger than me, but my pride got in the way of me walking away. I ended up taking a knock-out punch to the chin.

Another time I got whooped by a huge guy and his friends outside a 7-Eleven. After kicking my butt, he picked me up and threw me into the bushes, leaving me for dead. You'd think I would have had enough after that, but I couldn't let it go. After a few minutes, I sprang up while his back was turned. I kicked him in the small of his back, pushing him to the ground, and quickly started kicking him in the head while he was down.

When word got around, no one would fight me one-on-one. Groups of guys would jump me and surprise attack me from behind. This way of living was exhausting and painful, but I couldn't stop. Drugs and alcohol were a distraction from the hurt, but fighting was the real addiction. It was my life.

There are so many things I would rather forget, they are so difficult to remember. I didn't realize I had been held at gunpoint until

I heard about it happening to someone else. This was more recently, after I had left that old life far behind. The memory was completely unexpected, but my body physically remembered. I instantly got chills and broke out in a heart-pounding sweat. I could feel the cold metal gun barrel on the back of my neck. I realized I knew exactly what it felt like to have a gun cocked and shoved at the back of your head, to be powerless, defenseless, paralyzed. I remembered the beating well, but I never thought about the gun until then.

It happened one night when I got picked up by the cops. I can't recall why, maybe drunk in public. I was definitely drunk. I must have mouthed off to them because they started raging at me. "You think we can't do anything because of Rodney King? We'll show you motherf-----!" they yelled. I probably threatened them or said something stupid. This was during the time of the Rodney King riots, and it was all over the news. In fact, at the time, Roy was a National Guard reservist, and he was activated and sent to Los Angeles for the riots.

The two cops hogtied me with surprising speed before I knew what was happening. One of the officers picked up my thin nineteen-year-old body as if picking up a suitcase by the handle. It felt like my hands and feet were being ripped off. He threw me on my stomach in the back of their car. My face smashed into the side of the seat. My back arched in pain as my hands and feet were stretched impossibly tight behind my back. The handcuffs were pinching off my circulation. Being hogtied was agonizing and dehumanizing. I was screaming bloody murder and cussing at them to let me go. They drove me up to the east foothills to some deserted area, pulled me out of the car, and tossed me on the ground. **They kicked me around and beat me while I contorted in pain, my hands and feet still tied behind my back.**

They told me they would find me and kill me if I ever repeated what happened. One of the cops pulled his gun on me. "I'm not going down because of you, punk." My entire body instantly locked up, frozen, as he shoved his gun hard against the back of my skull. "I can kill you right now." I knew in that instant, he could. My body physically revolted with realization; my life was nothing, easily disposable. They dropped me off on the street afterwards. They never booked me or took me to the station. I couldn't process what had happened, but since I was alive, I guessed it didn't matter. I walked away in a stunned daze and pushed the incident completely out of mind, refusing to think about it until much later in life.

CHAPTER 16

The Pinta

I wanted to be out, but every time I was, real life was just too hard to handle.

On the morning of my eighteenth birthday, correctional officers walked me from Juvie over to the county jail across the street. I shuffled over in shackles, my juvenile-hall issued blue jeans, and my sweatshirt, carrying my transfer papers in cuffed hands. I was booked and admitted and handed the county jail orange top and beige pants. I was now an adult in jail.

There were so many times I took a bad plea deal. I didn't understand what I was admitting to. I was uneducated and often intimidated and pressured into bad plea bargains. I didn't have anyone to advocate for me who really cared. It was exhausting to try to defend myself, so I just caved.

I started a rock band with friends in my early twenties. We had a band called Grail and later Shaft. I was the lead singer. I liked the attention, but at the same time I was self-conscious. I worried a lot about my image and what people thought of me. We played local gigs, but we could never really make it because I was in and out of jail. No one could count on me so band members would come and go. I wrote songs to sing with my band, dreaming about making it big time. I remember thinking if I don't make something of my life in a few years, I'll just end it. I was trying to find my destiny, something deep and meaningful, but sadly the only thing I really excelled in was fighting. I was lost and drifting through life. When I was 21, I wrote a song called "Drifter."

I drift among dreams
You wallow in despair
It felt like I was being dragged
And no one even cared
I float on rotting driftwood
You choke yourself with sand
We both couldn't breathe
Til we fell on common land
It feels so wrong
Why did you go on?
You were so angry
And I thought that you were strong
I trouble myself with pleasure
You befriend pain
We were both hurting, but we have ourselves to blame
I walk down a dirt road

You walk down a paved

We both met at the end

And we found it was our grave

"Drifter" album cover when I remastered and released the song in 2021

under the band name Post Traumatic Quest

Singing in my band in my early twenties

In my mid-twenties, I got into a bar fight at the Cactus Club. My usual standard was stupidly to strike first and ask questions later. I was sitting at the bar when my friend ran up to tell me some guy was messing with Roy out front. The argument was still just verbal when I walked outside. They were in each other's faces shouting.

The guy's girlfriend was telling us to stop because he was an off-duty police officer. According to the police report, I allegedly replied, "I don't give a f---!" as I socked him in the face. I picked up a major assault case and was sent to prison for the first time.

When I was younger, I looked forward to going to prison in some deranged way. I thought it made me somebody, since my whole world was fighting. Now that I was there, I saw it was a disgusting, filthy place to be. I was brought to San Quentin State Prison Reception Center, north of San Francisco. Signs posted everywhere stated, "Warning Shots Will Not Be Fired." Although sometimes Mom would put money on my books, I never had a single visit when I was in prison. Everyone had given up on me years ago.

Upon arrival, I was placed in the general population, West Block. The cell that I shared with my bunky was about the same square footage as a king size bed with a toilet, sink, and bunk bed inside. I could sit on my bed and put my legs up against the opposite wall. There were limited shower heads for hundreds of men trying to shower in three minutes. There were two shower heads for the Mexicans, with five to ten of us quickly rotating between soaping and rinsing and one man standing guard. People would flood their cells trying to take bird baths to avoid the showers. Sometimes I did too. Growing up in the system, I have been permanently programmed to take extremely fast showers and scarf down my food like a beast. The food there was unrecognizable and tasteless. Dinner was early so you would go to bed hungry if you didn't have food in your cell.

What stands out the most about my time in prison is the noise. It was so loud the entire day long, putting you on edge and keeping stress levels high. Doors were always slamming. Men were fighting, screaming, and hollering constantly. I would sit for hours on end, unable to relax, trying to deal. It was hard not to lose your mind, especially when you heard other people ranting and raving and you knew they had really lost it. I honed my tuning-out skills to a fine art, which definitely came in handy whenever my mom or girlfriend nagged me.

It did get quiet for shut down at night. They beat you if you made any noise after that. The lights were always on, although slightly dimmer at night, and it was cramped, cold, and uncomfortable, so I was never rested.

I would sit for hours making pruno, popping hot meds, and writing poetry and songs. I worked out two to three hours a day. I did push-ups and burpees, but dips were my favorite. They cut and defined my chest so that I was in the best shape of my life. That's the weird thing about prison—you become super disciplined and regimented. In some ways it helps refine you as a person at the same time that it warps you and drives you insane.

Each time I was in prison, there had been a major gang fight just before I arrived, so we were on CTQ (Confined to Quarters) the whole time I was there. Sometimes we were on twenty-three-hour a day lockdown. I know this was God's grace helping me to avoid a hot yard where I could have really got in trouble. There was a point in my life I would have been willing to do anything to prove myself, and I would have lost my freedom forever. I have done time in San Quentin, Folsom, and Jamestown penitentiaries.

One morning at Jamestown, there was a huge commotion. Everyone rushed to the TV to see news of planes crashing into the World Trade Center. It was 9/11. At that time, I don't think I understood the gravity of that tragic day, but nevertheless a fear and panic began to overwhelm me. I felt powerless and lonely being locked up far away from my friends and family during a national tragedy.

In prison, I learned to shut down in order to cope. I turned off my emotions, numbed out, and buried everything so deep that even I didn't know what was going on inside me anymore. **I wanted to be out, but every time I was, real life was just too hard to handle.** Part of me thought it would be easier to just go back.

CHAPTER 17

Dancers and Dumpsters

I couldn't face my life or begin to deal with any of its basic responsibilities.

The first time I got out of prison I went into a work release program in Oakland for a couple months. The day I was released they handed me all the money I had accumulated—my two-hundred-dollar gate fee plus about eighteen hundred in wages. I went directly to the liquor store at the corner, about ten feet away from the Sober Living Environment Housing I had been living in. I bought a forty, jumped on BART, met up with my brother in San Jose, and went to a strip club. Strip clubs were commonplace, just the thing to do in the early 2000s. I spent more than half my money that night. When my friends left, I stayed behind talking to one of the dancers and got her number. We dated until I went back to prison, and on and off after that.

After the club, I had to walk home to a family member's house over ten miles away. I was freezing in only a t-shirt. I sat down by a dumpster to block the wind in an attempt to keep warm. I fell asleep or passed out for a while in the garbage area before I continued my long walk. This was what my life had come to. It was fun partying, and getting the dancer's number boosted my ego, but inside I knew I was really just another wasted bum sleeping on the street.

The next morning, I started smoking meth with friends and family at my relative's house. My hellish spiral of destruction lasted twenty-eight days. After less than a month, I was sent back to prison on an absconding charge. I never bothered to check in with my parole officer. I had been staying in a van parked at my grandpa's house. One afternoon we were hanging out in the backyard when armed police officers surrounded the house and arrested me.

The second time I was released from prison is a blur. I was released on a Friday and went back to jail on a Monday after doing a beer run. **I couldn't face my life or begin to deal with any of its basic responsibilities.** Being in jail was almost worse than prison, and I was there for eight months. The next time I violated my parole, I was sent to rehab.

CHAPTER 18

Crying Out to God in a Pool of Blood, From Death to Life

"And fear not them which kill the body but are not able to kill the soul: but rather fear him which is able to destroy both soul and body in hell."

Matthew 10:28

I was terrified to think about where I would go, shoving the thought out of my mind in revulsion.

My mom's cousin Eddy became a Christian after serving time. He went on to become a pastor. He tried to witness to me for years. Sometimes he would call me and talk and pray for what seemed like hours. I felt a little awkward around him now that he was born again. I would just sit there listening, drinking a beer while he went on and on. I didn't say anything because I didn't want to be disrespectful to a pastor, and I didn't know what he was talking about anyways.

When I left my last court ordered rehab early, my parole officer told me I had a month to find a new SLE (sober living environment). My Uncle Eddy said I could stay in the dorms on the church property in exchange for working there, attending all services, and keeping my nose clean. I stopped by the church to make the plans and went to the college night service.

The college pastor was Simon Woodstock. He formerly had a crazy life as a professional skateboarder and MTV VJ. I always thought he was an awesome skateboarder, and I used to watch his crazy antics on television. I knew he partied pretty hard, so I was shocked to meet him at church and find out he was a pastor. After talking to him, I could see that he was really into God and studying the Bible and that he seemed to genuinely care about me. I thought that if he could change then probably just about anyone could.

Part of me was starting to be a little hopeful that this could actually work for me. That feeling quickly left me as I exited the building though, just as it had the few other times I visited church. I ended up going on an insane binge in San Francisco. I returned to my mom's house hungover and in a panic, knowing I was scheduled for a drug test I couldn't pass. I decided to take baking soda because it is said to help clear your system. I got so sick, with excruciating stomach pains and uncontrollable vomiting. I felt like I was dying.

I realized in horror I didn't just feel like I was dying, I really was.

The vomiting turned into wrenching up what looked like liters of dark red blood. I filled the entire sink, three times over. I broke into a clammy, cold sweat, convulsing in pain and utter fear in the empty house. I was dizzy as a black fog closed in on my vision. I felt like I would pass out any second, and I doubted I would ever wake up.

All the years I toyed with dying, I liked the *idea* of death. Now I thought maybe I had never known what life was really about. I found I didn't want to die at all. I wanted to live, even as I could feel life draining out of me.

I thought about things I had heard about heaven and hell. Worse than the pain I was experiencing now was contemplating eternity. I was afraid to consider the permanence and finality of death after the choices I had made. **I was terrified to think about where I would go, shoving the thought out of my mind in revulsion.**

I remembered hearing the message of salvation: Jesus said, *"I am the way and the truth and the life. No one comes to the Father except through me"* (John 14:6). *"For the wages of sin is death; but the gift of God is eternal life through Jesus Christ our Lord"* (Romans 6:23).

I needed a Savior. I cried out to God from the depths of my heart and tears rolled down my cheeks. I didn't know what to say except for "Help me!" He did. A strong will for life welled up in my spirit. The pain gradually eased. A quiet peace came over me, and later I was able to fall asleep. I was miraculously fine after that, and I continued to detox the next couple days with only moderate symptoms. God immediately set me free from the bondage of alcohol and drugs that had enslaved me for so many years. God gave me that freedom, and I did my part of drawing near to Him and resisting evil.

The following week, I walked onto the church premises with a black garbage bag full of all my belongings and a hundred dollars Mom had given me. That was all I had in this world. I moved into the dorms with other young men and started working around the church facilities.

Without a second thought, I made drastic changes to every aspect of my life. I stopped hanging out with my old friends, broke up with the girlfriend I met in rehab and that dancer I had been seeing, and totally immersed myself in the Word of God through reading the Bible. This was different from my false conversion in jail. I was so happy my life had been saved that I didn't care what anyone said or thought about me. I didn't care if I looked crazy. I was finally living.

Change requires a lot of courage. I respect anyone who does the hard work of recovery, therapy, or treatment. You have to be brave enough to look at yourself and admit your life isn't working. You have to be humble enough to seek help. You have to set boundaries and change your habits. I completely changed my mindset and my entire way of living. I had to go way outside my comfort zone in almost every area of my life.

I had hope now, and I walked around with a huge grin, singing and chatting with everyone I encountered. I wanted to tell everyone what Jesus did for me. I would read my Bible day and night, and I could feel my mind growing stronger each day. Living in the church dorm, I was constantly around caring people who encouraged me. The church people certainly weren't perfect, and there were other types of pettiness and problems, but I was oblivious to all that. I was so happy to be in a safe, loving, and positive environment. I realize now it gave me structure without formal rules. The various weekly gatherings kept me busy almost every day as well as my work and responsibilities. I immersed myself in this new church world and did everything I could to adapt to my new environment. I was high on life.

I discovered God's love, peace, and truth, an entirely new way of interacting with the world. I developed a relationship with God as my Father. He was my Father in very practical ways, providing me with a roof over my head, a job, food, and friendship with healthy families in our church.

I made my child support payments and visited my kids. I got my driver's license for the first time in my life at age thirty. I had been driving since I was a teenager, and even previously owned a scooter and a motorcycle, but I had never driven legally. I discovered a joy in working hard every day. I woke up early to read my Bible and pray, work all day, go to Bible studies in the evenings, and roll into bed physically exhausted, falling asleep as soon as my head hit the pillow. It felt great.

The church provided a family environment that really supported me. There were people that took me under their wing and invested in me. They showed me generosity and care. One friend took me to Men's Warehouse and bought me my first suit. I couldn't believe he wanted to spend that kind of money on me. Families would have me over for dinner. Some of the guys that worked construction would take me along for occasional side jobs so I could earn some extra money. It was fun working with them and going out to eat afterwards.

This became a big part of what I do with my students today. Hanging out together, having fun, and eating is how you get to know each other. As I continued taking small, daily steps toward this new way of life, the more optimistic, comfortable, and confident I became. I started to believe the people around me really did care and wanted to see me succeed. I began to dream again. Maybe there was a great future out there for me. Accepting God's love allowed me to see everything differently.

I could talk for hours with all different types of people in my church because we all loved the Lord. This taught me I could connect with absolutely anyone through the lens of love. Uncle Eddy kept on me. He was extremely strict, and I worked my butt off to please him and show I was grateful. I continued living in the dorms and working the grounds.

I took Bible college classes, classes on theology, Greek, and apologetics. I studied everything I could get my hands on and found I enjoyed it. I learned how to study and prepare sermons. I went on to become the facilities manager, youth minister volunteer, and then an ordained pastor.

CHAPTER 19

Wedding Bells in Reno

"'For I know the plans I have for you,' declares the LORD, 'plans to prosper you and not to harm you, plans to give you hope and a future. Then you will call upon me and come and pray to me, and I will listen to you. You will seek me and find me when you seek me with all your heart. I will be found by you,' declares the LORD, 'and will bring you back from captivity.'"

Jeremiah 29:11–14

I felt strongly compelled to reach youth in the same situation I had been in. It was my quest.

After a couple of years living in the dorms and working as a gardener at the church and the elementary school that was on campus, I met my future wife. She was a single mom named

Abby. She attended our church, and her son, Solomon, was a kin-dergartner at the school. I would see her drop her son off for school early in the morning when I was working the campus. She would be dressed up for work in heels and a pencil skirt, and her long red hair caught my eye. I smiled and said good morning, trying to keep it holy and not stare.

Abby went on a church trip to Israel with a close friend of mine who got to know her on the tour and had us both over for a bar-beque. We were the only single people there, so it was basically a set up. I had spoken to her briefly a couple times but never had the chance to really sit down and talk. We ended up having a long con-versation and an immediate connection. After that we were pretty much inseparable.

As soon as we started dating, I knew I should get tested for STDs. I really cared about Abby, and I figured I should get the test out of the way before she invested any more time into the relation-ship. I tried not to worry while I waited for the results, but I was so nervous, and a crippling fear consumed my mind. I thought about how many people I had slept with, how many tattoos I had gotten in prison.

By the undeserving grace of God, all the test results were nega-tive. Not only did I not have the dreaded HIV, I didn't have hepati-tis either, which is almost guaranteed after getting tattoos in prison. The same anxious thoughts flooded my mind when I took another test for insurance purposes a few years later, but again I was all clear. I felt so blessed and at the same time truly humbled.

We knew we wanted to get married, but a wedding seemed far off in the future. We prayed and fasted about our relationship. I went to a jeweler and put a deposit down on a beautiful ring I picked out for her. In an impulsive moment, we flew to Reno and got married after only six weeks of dating! Some people thought it was because we had slept together before marriage (which was against our Christian values), but we hadn't. We did wait until our wedding night, but we didn't want to wait a long time to get married. We had a small ceremony at our church two weeks later.

Because of our hasty decision, we had an avalanche of issues to work out. Abby had a five-year-old son who lived with us full time. I had shared custody and visitation with my fourteen-year-old son and six-year-old daughter. We had to deal with the demands of blending a family in addition to a lot of hurt from our pasts and destructive patterns from previous relationships and wounds.

A brand-new marriage after a short courtship, blending a step-family, high cost living in Silicon Valley, and working at a church in full-time ministry would have made life hard for anyone. It was especially difficult for me because I was ill equipped to meet all the demands and because of past trauma. We felt a lot of pressure to always act like things were great, being on church staff. Abby and I tried to hold things together and do our best, but we made a lot of mistakes. We regrettably put pressure and strict rules on our kids because of the demands we felt.

Later on, in my crisis response training, I learned about Post Traumatic Stress Disorder. I realized that due to my past, I experienced many PTSD symptoms, especially during the beginning of our marriage. That led to a lot of arguing and tough challenges; because of that we had to dig deep. It is a continuous process and has taken time, but we have developed a profound intimacy on an emotional, mental, physical, and spiritual level. Of course, we still have disagreements, and difficult and painful times, but we are continuously growing and enjoying the life we build together.

When we married in 2005, I continued to volunteer in our church's junior high ministry and Abby joined me. I went on to become the youth pastor and served in numerous functions and ministries in our church.

During our years of student ministry, there were lots of youth winter and summer camps in addition to our weekly gatherings. We crammed everyone into the old church bus through winding mountain roads to get to camp, taking roll call at every stop. There was no air conditioning in the bus, and we would drive for hours to southern California during the summer. We had overnight lock-ins every New Year's Eve, where the high schoolers would stay up all night at the church. We would play the game "murder in the dark" in the large 1970s church sanctuary. We would have a sermon and worship music and planned games and activities that lasted until the morning. All this was fueled by massive amounts of junk food and candy.

Abby and I also led the addiction and recovery ministry together for a few years. Abby picked up women twice a week from a local rehab facility. I would stay late talking to the men, wanting to be there for everyone. It was therapeutic for me to lead the recovery ministry, but I was unintentionally developing some bad habits in my aim to give back. I was at church all the time, endlessly working. I didn't know how to say no, slow down, rest, or even be truly present with my family much of the time.

While we now had three children combined, Abby and I really wanted a baby together and worried about how we could afford it. Abby, Solomon, and I lived in a tiny two-bedroom, one-bathroom apartment, with Daniel and Minna visiting every other weekend. Money was tight.

After a couple years of marriage, we were able to join a first-time home buyer program. Being a homeowner in the Bay Area was unthinkable to me, but Abby and I began to dream of it together. We were shocked when the loan officer approved us on the spot, and we were able to buy a condo with more room. It was truly a miracle after all my court fees, debt, and unstable job history to say the least. We worked closely with the loan officer through the processes and she ended up coming to our church, getting saved, and asking me to baptize her!

We were thrilled to be homeowners, but our new mortgage payment stretched us even more financially, making our dream of having a baby seem hopeless. We wanted Abby to be able to stay home with the new baby at least for a couple years, but it would be impossible for us to survive without her income. We prayed about what to do.

During the time we were praying about having a baby, we went on a mission trip to Mexico to work at an orphanage. I had been there a few years in a row, but this was Abby's first time coming with me. The orphanage had children that lived there full time, and they also served many children who were left alone during the day. Young children of working parents are often left alone due to lack of childcare. The orphanage buses them in, feeds them breakfast and lunch, and provides free schooling and activities.

The area the volunteers stayed in didn't have real showers, so we had to fill up buckets with water and soap down. There was a separate men's side and women's side for sleeping, large rooms filled with bunk beds. We brought our own sleeping bags to lay on the thin mattresses. The generator shut off at 10 p.m. and everything went completely dark. We mixed cement, painted, or worked on different construction projects part of the days. Other times we took the orphanage bus on the bumpy unpaved roads to shantytowns where mangy dogs roamed around. We would invite the kids to come to the daycare center for snacks and activities.

We loved meeting all the kids. Abby fell in love with one little preschool age girl named Daniela. Abby could communicate with her pretty well in Spanish. I, on the other hand, repeatedly disappointed people because they automatically assumed I could speak Spanish, but I couldn't at all. Daniela would hold Abby's hand and sit on her lap. Abby and I caught eyes and we knew we had to step out in faith to have a baby of our own.

A couple months after that trip Abby was pregnant. After almost four years of marriage, we were expecting a baby girl. I was blessed to be involved and present every step of the way during the pregnancy. We had fun setting up and decorating her room. We received so many gifts that our daughter was set on clothes for a least a year.

Shortly before the due date, we went to one last appointment. It was with a midwife at El Camino Hospital, as Abby had her heart set on natural childbirth. After the appointment, we went out for lunch at one of our favorite restaurants, The Fish Market. It was a splurge for us at the time, even though we were supposed to be buckling down to save money. We talked about the news we had heard at the appointment—the baby could come at any time. We were excited, but the conversation turned to our financial struggles and our dream of Abby being able to stay home with the new baby. It seemed impossible.

I got up to go to the restroom. Some random guy in the bathroom started asking me about the tattoos on my neck. I thought it was strange. He started trying to share the gospel with me. I told him I was already a believer; in fact, I was a pastor. It turned out the guy was the author of a book I had read about witnessing to people and leading them to Christ. He happened to be in San Jose for a conference.

I went back to our table and told Abby who I had just met. When we finished and asked for the check, the server told us the check had already been paid. The evangelist guy had paid for our meal. Abby and I looked at each other and our eyes welled up with tears. We knew God was encouraging us and letting us know everything would be ok.

A day or two later, Abby went into labor. I tried to be as helpful and supportive as I could. After hours of labor, it was finally time for our baby to be born. The midwife called me closer and told me to put out my hand. I was shocked to realize the reason she asked me to put out my hand was so that I could catch my daughter as she was being born! I was completely caught off guard and stood there stunned as I saw this fragile little baby take her first breath and heard her first tiny cry.

In a daze, I placed her carefully on Abby. The midwife stood back, letting me know this intimate moment was just about the three of us: me, Abby, and our baby. Next the nurses helped me cut the cord. It was something I had heard about, but I always thought was kind of weird or gross. It was actually an incredible experience, being part of the birth in such a hands-on way. I was able to be present, instead of being hungover, out of it, or just caught up with myself. Everything was different now.

Staring into my daughter's eyes shortly after her birth

We named her Michal-Donna. Michal is a princess in the Bible, daughter of King Saul and wife of King David. Donna is after Abby's mom, a beautiful, godly woman who passed away when Abby was a child. Having a new baby again after so many years was a completely different and beautiful experience for both of us. We were both kids ourselves, young and immature, when our other children from past relationships were born. Now, at 36, I was in a totally different place in my life. We had a chance to start over as parents and learn from our previous mistakes.

Michal-Donna and me

When we first brought Michal-Donna home from the hospital, family and friends were waiting at our house to welcome us. Solomon and Abby's sister Rachel had set things up and prepared lunch. One of the friends was holding Michal-Donna on our couch. I asked her to get up and move because there was a big mirror hanging on the wall where she was sitting. I was afraid it would fall on the baby if there was an earthquake. It's kind of laughable now, but having this little newborn made me hyperaware of all the potential dangers around us. I was always double-checking doors, making sure she was breathing okay, and checking on her multiple times a night. I would get especially anxious about things being anywhere near her neck. Even when she grew to elementary school age, I never wanted her wearing a necklace or a scarf. I unknowingly projected my anxiety onto her.

When Michal-Donna was almost a year old, Abby went back to work part time for a short period. When she was required to go back full time, she ended up resigning, and somehow, we were able to make it work on one income. A year and a half later, our son Jonah was born. Our family was complete.

Dad, Jonah, and me

Through my job as a youth pastor, I began organizing large events at our church like music concerts and skate contests. Our church didn't branch out much into the local community, or even with other local churches, so I made it my mission to change that. These events began drawing in lots of other people, which I liked to see. I would pass out flyers at different skate shops and connect with youth pastors at other churches. I promoted the events and ran advertisements on Christian radio stations. I was constantly on the go and making plans for the next big event. I was gaining a lot of useful knowledge and experience. I loved working with the bands, artists, and professional skaters. I learned about riders (requests from the bands). I would make sure our staff set up the green room to meet the specific needs of each band. I would often take the musicians out to eat or show them around the Bay Area, taking them to San Francisco or Santa Cruz. It was a fun and exciting time for our family, but I also neglected them in many ways. I left Abby to manage things because I was so busy working.

Around this time, I began volunteering on The City of San Jose Mayor's Gang Prevention Task force. I attended every meeting and event and tried to help wherever I saw a need. I couldn't just sit back in my church office. I needed to be out in the community connecting with people.

When I was in the hospital after being stabbed, I was able to see how messed up my life really was. I wish someone would have intervened at that critical moment. I was so scared when it first happened that I would have listened to just about anyone. I wanted change, but I didn't think that was even a possibility or an option. My identity was wrapped up in this violent world where the ultimate outcome was either death or imprisonment. I didn't know what it was to be an adult or see beyond to a better life.

Instead of showing kids the inside of a prison as a scare tactic, I want to show them how fulfilling life can be. I want to get them out of the confinement of their hood and show them life can be so much better than they can even dream. I know God has a plan for these kids. **I felt strongly compelled to reach youth in the same situation I had been in. It was my quest.** That burning passion led me to develop the volunteer Community Chaplain Crisis Response program with the assistance of others. The program supports victims and families after a gang related homicide or injury.

As a volunteer for the program, I was notified when there was a stabbing or shooting and would go to visit the victim in the hospital. I would talk to them, encourage them, meet their families, provide any help I could offer, and do what I could to stay connected or refer them to another chaplain. It wasn't a one-size-fits-all approach. I had built relationships over the years with a large number of ministers from different denominations, affiliations, and backgrounds, and with different types of community-based organizations. I could make referrals that suited them best.

Tragically I was also called when there had been a homicide. It was heart-wrenching to walk with the families through the pain. When needed, we did what we could to gather donations from various churches to help pay for costly burial and funeral arrangements. Some churches would donate their time and facilities for the services, and some would donate financially. Many times, there was a little brother or cousin I was drawn to. I prayed they would make the right choices and their life would take a different path.

CHAPTER 20

From the Big House to the White House

"Now all glory to God, who is able, through his mighty power at work within us, to accomplish infinitely more than we might ask or think."

Ephesians 3:20

My record had been hanging over our heads. God was bringing it to the surface now to show me that there was no door that was closed to me if He chose to open it.

It was a morning like any other at the church office when I was told I had a call from the Department of Justice in Washington D.C. I had been nominated and chosen to be honored as a Champion of Change at the White House! My excitement quickly turned to panic when I was informed that my criminal record could prevent me from being allowed to go. I had to wait two excruciatingly long weeks in limbo before I could find out if I was granted clearance.

All of my horrendous past charges came to mind. I was embarrassed, filled with shame. I was such a different person now, my past seemed like another lifetime, and I didn't want my record to hold me back from the work I was doing now. I already had a deep remorse for the people I hurt, but now I felt haunted.

I had realized years before that while there would still be consequences, Jesus set me free and bore all my guilt on the cross. I had to fight off the lies of the enemy that were putting me back in the chains of my past. The Lord showed me it was precisely because of my past that I had this opportunity at all. He works all things together for my good (Romans 8:28). God doesn't do bad things to us, but He is the one who can take the mess that we've made and turn it around.

II Corinthians 12:9–10 encouraged me: *"And He said to me, 'My grace is sufficient for you, for My strength is made perfect in weakness.' Therefore, most gladly I will rather boast in my infirmities, that the power of Christ may rest upon me. Therefore, I take pleasure in infirmities, in reproaches, in needs, in persecutions, in distresses, for Christ's sake. For when I am weak, then I am strong."*

Abby and I prayed and left the outcome in God's hands. We have seen Him do so many miracles in our lives, and we know that He always has our very best interest in mind. **My record had been hanging over our heads. God was bringing it to the surface now to show me that there was no door that was closed to me if He chose to open it.** I could go anywhere He chose to take me, and there was nothing that could stand in my way, not even my shameful past. In the coming years, I went on to get most of my record expunged and was granted a certificate of rehabilitation.

When we finally found out I was cleared to go, the Champion of Change trip was a whirlwind of last-minute travel plans, childcare arrangements, and preparation. We flew to Washington for only one night. It was a fast-paced, exhausting trip, but it was also the experience of a lifetime. Abby and I had never been to D.C. before, so we walked around until 1 a.m. sightseeing and visiting the different monuments.

The next day we toured the White House, and I met the eleven other outstanding men and women who were being recognized for their work in youth violence prevention. I noticed everyone and their guests all had green badges, but mine was bright pink. I guess my clearance was different, and I had been flagged because of my record. I got so nervous every time we came up to a new gate or checkpoint, and there were many, but my escort continuously waved me through. Thank God I was allowed to go!

Abby and me at the White House, April 2012

I was introduced to people rapidly and tried to keep track of all the names and impressive titles. Everyone was so well dressed and there were tons of bright young interns in business suits. They looked so young with their baby faces but were brisk and articulate like they had been doing this for years.

The award was personally signed by President Barack Obama. At first, we were told that he would be there to present the awards, but then we were told he couldn't make it. Right up until the last minute, we weren't completely sure if he would be in room. Not good for my nerves.

After we were shown around, it was time to meet with the press. I sat on the panel with the other honorees. The Associate Attorney General from the Department of Justice was there to present the questions to us.

A hush fell over the room. The occasional click and flash of a camera seemed to echo. The first question was addressed to me. I was caught off guard but managed to bumble through that first answer. I had no idea how to prepare or train for this new experience. I hoped they would come back to me for another question so I could have a chance to redeem myself. Thankfully, they did. I hoped my second answer made more sense.

Fumbling through that first question made me realize I needed to step up my public speaking game. I began to make that a priority, which launched my career. I had never really traveled before in my life, but in the years after my award from the President, more doors were opened to me. I feel truly blessed and so grateful for every opportunity.

When I returned home, I was given a commendation from the Mayor and the City of San Jose. I accepted the award in the City

Hall Rotunda. I expressed the point that though I was once destructive, I now strive to build, and my passion is to serve my community. My heart swelled as it struck me how true those words were. My family watched from their seats and clapped. Grandpa and Grandma Phillips, Abby's grandparents, were there with huge smiles on their faces. I could feel God leading me into this new world. He was helping me to rise to the occasion. It was intimidating to be in this new environment of government officials and leaders, but I knew God would give me the confidence. He was showing me a greater vision for my life.

Who would have thought an uneducated convict would be speaking at our nation's capital to community leaders from all across the country and receiving an award in San Jose City Hall? God knew all along. Although both of my grandmothers had passed away many years earlier, I could feel the love of their prayers. For so many years I lived an empty life, never thinking about how I could help others. God gave me purpose.

As protocol, I was sent to the next of kin of a recent homicide victim. I walked into the apartment complex of the grieving family. The young man had been loved by many; there were a ton of people at the home. As I walked up, the garage was open, and there were about forty young men gathered there, all active gang members. I could feel the tension. I was a stranger there. I always carry a big Bible with me so it's obvious I am there as a pastor, to offer support. The apartment was in the neighborhood of the rival gang.

Here were all these guys hanging out right in the hood of the rival gang, the gang who had killed their friend. I knew it was a dangerous situation.

When I went inside there was food everywhere. Everyone wanted to show their love. I spoke with the mother of the young man who had been killed, and when she welcomed and accepted me, it led her son to accept me also. Once the brother acknowledged me, his friends were okay with me being there.

I prayed with the family and friends and offered resources. On my way out, I stopped in front of the garage to say goodbye to the group of young men. They were drinking and passing around joints. My heart went out to them. I knew they were mourning the loss of their friend, their brother. I could feel their anger too. He had been stabbed over 30 times and left to die in the street.

I heard loud music blaring and turned to see a car full of rival gang members driving inside the apartment complex with rags hanging out the window. They were creeping down the street real slow, blasting their music, making their presence known. Here I was standing right in the middle of two rival gangs in a heated situation. I had a lady from church with me as a Spanish interpreter, and I prayed we weren't about to find ourselves in the middle of a shooting. Thankfully they kept on driving, probably because there were so many people around. I thanked God no one else lost their life in that moment.

The following year I got a call from the city late on a Sunday night, requesting my service as a chaplain. I was told there was a large crowd beginning to gather at the spot where their loved one had been murdered, and they were flashing their colors and rags. They didn't want to escalate the situation by sending the police, but they were worried it could lead to more violence. Abby was upset that they were sending me into a dangerous situation late at night. We prayed and decided I should wear a suit and bring my big Bible to show that I was there as clergy.

The victim had been shot in front of a 7-Eleven on the corner of a busy street. The family made a memorial for him there with his picture and rags. I spoke with them and heard the grief and pain they were experiencing. I gently explained the concern about the rags drawing unwanted attention and asked if they would respectfully consider taking them down. They agreed to remove them. I stayed around until the crowd began to disperse and thankfully nothing else happened.

CHAPTER 21

Passion Project Hustle, the Birth of The City Peace Project

My quest had brought me to this, becoming an agent of peace instead of violence.

I studied everything I could get my hands on; attended numerous conferences, trainings, and classes in youth mentorship, anti-bullying, and peer support; and completed certifications as a crisis first responder. My years of experience as a hospital and community chaplain and cultivating close relationships in my community gave me the real skills and expertise. I often relived my pain when helping others through theirs. In those times, it was healing for me to try to share the love and support I needed when I was in a similar situation. I was able to express my thanks to God and to those that helped me by helping others.

Due to circumstances outside my control, I found myself laid off and out of work. I had four young children at the time. My wife hadn't been working since the birth of our last baby, and we lived paycheck to paycheck. I could have pursued a job at another large church as an associate or youth pastor, but I knew I had to follow my heart. I needed to do something beyond a job. It was something I had to do no matter what.

I decided to start my own non-profit organization. We started with weekly Bible study and church services in addition to community events and outreach. We did peace prayer walks, neighborhood clean-ups, mural projects, and food drives. We also volunteered at late night gyms, which gave local youth a fun, safe place to hang out. Late night gyms were organized as a gang prevention tool as a way to keep kids off the street and support them in a positive way. I loved hanging out with the kids there, playing handball, eating pizza, and chatting it up with them.

Abby's grandparents, Dr. Don and Ruthanne Phillips, and a few other friends and family members were supportive from day one. Without their love and support, it wouldn't have been possible. Grandpa and Grandma Phillips always prayed for us and encouraged us. They donated toward the start-up fees to help get us off the ground and legally incorporated. They attended all our events, and cheered us on. They fully supported the start-up of my new career and ministry.

Grandpa Don understood pivoting from traditional church ministry to follow your heart's dream. He worked in church ministry as an ordained pastor for many years before getting a PhD as a psychologist and becoming a licensed marriage and family therapist. He was the first chaplain on staff for Santa Clara County's juvenile hall in the 1960s and a wise and loving mentor to me.

Grandma constantly bragged on me to anyone that would listen and kept printouts of any articles I was featured in. Grandma was a teacher for over 40 years and worked at Santee Elementary and Franklin-McKinley School District. The schools she worked in are some of the most underserved in San Jose, so Grandma knew the schools and community I worked with well. She loved that community and loved to hear all about my work. Both Grandpa and Grandma only saw my good points, never my flaws. They celebrated even my most insignificant achievements. They woke up early every morning to cover each family member in prayer. They prayed for each of us by name.

Grandpa would oftentimes type up his prayers and give them to us. He printed out a beautiful prayer for Jonah the day before he was born. Jonah came a little early. We knew he would be born soon, but we didn't know it would be right after Grandpa wrote that prayer. There were also two earthquakes, one even happening while Abby was in labor at the hospital. We have Grandpa's prayer and blessing framed in Jonah's bedroom. My wife's grandparents were the most supportive, loving, and steadfast influence I have ever known.

Ruthanne Phillips and Dr. Don Phillips when I received the Movers of Mountains Award
by the Dr. Martin Luther King Jr. Association of Santa Clara County (October 2013)

Jonah was born in 2011. In December 2012, Abby and I founded the non-profit. After a brief brainstorming session, Abby came up with the name: The City Peace Project. **My quest had brought me to this, becoming an agent of peace instead of violence.** Through God's love and forgiveness, I was able to face my pain and use it as my purpose in life by helping others. Through living out my life's purpose, I found peace.

Over the years, the mission of The City Peace Project has changed and developed. At first, we were meeting the immediate needs of homicide victims, and gradually we were able to take on more preventative work, including coaching, mentoring, tech tours at major Silicon Valley tech companies, and student ally groups.

I was invited to give the invocation (opening prayer) for the San Jose Mayor's final State of the City Address. It was held in February 2014 at the San Jose McEnery Convention Center downtown. It is a huge venue. There were press everywhere. I saw many familiar faces and was introduced to many new ones as I mingled in the VIP area before the event. I felt like the air was charged with excitement. I was nervous, understanding what an honor it was, but I knew I was prepared this time. I had rehearsed over and over for weeks. They introduced me as I came up to the mic and asked the crowd to join me in prayer. I could feel God's strength carrying me through and the prayers and love of family and friends supporting me.

Here is a portion of that prayer:

We marvel that just 150 years ago we were a small farming community and yet now we are the third largest city in California, the tenth largest city in the United States, the heart of the Silicon Valley, and one of the most influential places to live in the world.

We know that the true state of our city depends on how those of us in this diverse metropolis will choose to labor together, learn together, and live together.

From the offices of city hall to the streets of our inner city.

From the great glory of the Silicon Valley to the corners of every neighborhood.

From the pinnacles of technology and innovation, to the hallways and classrooms of every school.

We know there is still work to be done.

So might we continue to ease the pain of the homeless,

the hopeless, the exploited, the children that are lost and hurting.

We never want our great accomplishments to remove us from their pain.

We remember them, O Lord, and promise to link arms on their behalf.

God bless our city, San Jose, in Jesus name. Amen

I stepped down from the stage and took my seat. I could breathe easy now that it was over, knowing I had done my best. Because it was the Mayor's final State of the City Address, his children were able to share a touching tribute. It was a great event. We were kept late talking to everyone afterwards. Eventually we made it home to relieve the babysitter. I was very happy and very tired. I walked through my front door to see my two youngest children, ages three and four, sleeping peacefully on the couch.

Before we could rest, I received a familiar but still heart wrenching phone call. I was called to the hospital for a young man that had been shot. I walked right back out the door I had just walked in, still in my suit, but now with a heavy heart. I was there to pray and support the mother, father, and younger siblings as they received the death notification. It turned out I knew the family. They lived on the same street as my grandpa. I felt a renewed urgency to see an end to the violence in my city.

San Jose is one of the safest big cities in the nation. At one time, it was the number one safest big city, then fell to number six and continues to fluctuate. It is so safe that many don't realize what a big city it is and think of it more as a suburb. It is actually significantly larger than its neighboring San Francisco and Oakland, with over a million residents. Compared to other cities of that size, the homicide, violence, and crime rates are low. Violence tends to spike during the summer when kids are out of school and people stay out late. There was a horrible spike in 2012 when the death toll reached 46. A huge majority of those deaths took place during a two-week period in the summer. Not all the homicides that year were gang related, but it was the most violence we'd seen in over 20 years.

Thankfully, things have since calmed down and we haven't seen another spike like that. Being a volunteer member of The Mayor's Gang Prevention Task Force, we strategize on ways to bring down the homicide rate. I feel the impact of each one personally.

Often times I end up having a direct connection to the family. There have been many times when I'm called to meet with a family, and we come to find we know each other from the past or have mutual friends or relatives in common.

CHAPTER 22

Tel Aviv, Tequila, and Tech

Eventually I found some common ground, a way to connect—trauma. Pain is the great common denominator.

In early 2015, I was invited to be a part of Latinosphere, a delegation of Hispanic entrepreneurs on a trip to Israel. When I first heard about the opportunity, I panicked and didn't know if I should go. I had less than twelve hours to make my decision, and the pressure made me even more anxious. They had someone else lined up who would gladly take my place if I wanted to pass. I had never been overseas or on a plane ride that long. "Of course, you should go. I want to come too!" was Abby's reply. She never hesitated for a moment. She seemed so casual about it. That eased some of my anxiety, but I was still extremely nervous. My aunts and uncles and all the kids I worked with were afraid I would get kidnapped by ISIS.

We paid out of pocket for Abby's portion of the trip, and they allowed her to join. My mom stayed with the kids, making the trip possible for us. Abby booked our flights and planned the most amazing six hours in Amsterdam, where we had a layover on the way there.

We knew our time was limited, so when we landed in Amsterdam, we hurried off the plane, walking quickly to the lockers where we stored our carry-ons. I kept pace with Abby as we made a bee-line for the ticket kiosk, bought our tickets, and hopped on the train into the city.

It was so weird to find myself in a European country for the first time. I tried to be cool and not stand out as a tourist. We visited every single site on Abby's list by foot. It felt good to do all that walking after hours of being cramped in coach with no leg room.

We went to a huge castle-looking museum, Rijksmuseum, where I spotted a skate ramp. Tons of young guys were crowded there trying to find room to skate on it. I wished I had my board with me. We had a romantic coffee date at Café Americain. You could feel the history of the art and stained-glass windows. And later I got to try a pickled herring sandwich and fries with curry sauce.

Our second plane touched down in Tel Aviv. When we deboarded the plane, there was a man in a tailored suit holding a sign that said SANCHEZ right outside the door. He was tall with a professional appearance and looked like very serious security—like a military guy, or maybe FBI. He wasn't standing in the terminal of the airport, but on the actual passenger boarding bridge immediately outside the door of the plane. He took our baggage as he introduced himself and escorted us to an executive car waiting right on the tarmac. We drove to another wing of the airport so we didn't have to waste any time walking through. We were ushered straight to the front of the passport line. Our guide took our passports directly to the counter. We really got the royal treatment being guests of the Israeli Ministry of Foreign Affairs!

Our driver chatted it up with us and told us about the celebrities he had escorted in the past. He said he had worked with Madonna several times. He knew San Jose and the Bay Area well. He had a house in Los Gatos.

He asked us if we wanted to take advantage of the ATM while we were there. We tried to hide the fact that we were really low on funds before payday. We pulled out some cash thinking it was $100, but it was only around $25. We went back to the ATM, but we were scared to take out too much cash and accrue overdraft fees. We must have looked so dumb. He probably laughed to himself while we went back and forth. Here we were getting VIP treatment and we were broke. How embarrassing.

Once we arrived in Jerusalem after an overnight in Tel Aviv, we couldn't wait to get out and see everything. We rushed out of the lobby of our hotel into the Old City. We had no idea where we were going and got caught up in a tangle of tiny shops winding through narrow stone streets. Light rain began to fall, and we didn't know how to get out of the maze. We tried asking someone. A little old lady who didn't speak English motioned for us to follow her. She was surprisingly nimble, and we picked up our pace to follow after her. I fell on my butt walking down a slippery stone mini ramp. I brushed it off and hurried to keep up. We turned corner after corner wondering if she understood what we had asked. She nodded and kept motioning for us to follow. We came up to a courtyard, and she stretched out her hand, presenting a church to us. We thanked her and walked inside.

We fell silent as we stepped into the tangibly holy atmosphere. We saw people who were noticeably from all over the world, bringing cloths to rub on a stone slab as they wept quietly, tears falling down their cheeks. You could sense how sacred this place was. We figured out later it was the Church of the Holy Sepulchre. This is believed to be the place where Jesus' body was prepared for burial. We were very moved to see the tears and reverence of all the pilgrims who had traveled from afar to be here.

The next morning, I got down to business. I had a full schedule packed with meetings. I felt nakedly out of place in the meetings among all the entrepreneurs. I had been invited as a social entrepreneur, while everyone else had tech and business backgrounds with extremely impressive resumes. They used tech jargon and lingo I couldn't even pretend to keep up with. I barely got my GED in Elmwood County Jail. I sat in the meetings nodding my head with a big smile on my face, because I didn't know what else to do. I tried not to doze off, but the jet leg made me drowsy anytime I sat still for very long.

Eventually I found some common ground, a way to connect—
trauma. Pain is the great common denominator. Was that how I
could contribute among all these awe-inspiring people? Was that
why God brought me here? I was privileged to meet an Israeli Navy
Seal Commander and hostage negotiator, director at NATAL—the
Israel Trauma and Resiliency Center. He was also a clinical psychologist. He explained how virtually every person in Israel is at potential risk of psychological trauma. Military service is compulsory for
most students graduating high school, and living under continuous
threat of terror and war gives way to long-term impact. Instead of
hiding the trauma or creating stigma around treatment, they have
created a culture of acceptance of counseling, which leads to resiliency. They view PTSD survivors as heroes, not victims. Survivors
are encouraged to seek treatment and then help others through their
trauma, becoming heroes to those they help. Helping others is what
got me through my pain. I could totally relate.

I already knew we desperately needed to create a culture of
openness, acceptance, and healing back home, and this experience
really validated that. Many of my students were dealing with their
own versions of terror and war.

Abby did her own thing while I was in my business meetings.
At night we would walk around exploring or grab a late-night snack
at a little hole in the wall restaurant. One night, while we were walking around, I noticed a group of skaters. I saw them walk into a
skate shop near our hotel that I hadn't noticed before. We went in
and chatted with the owner. I noticed a picture of a pro skater from
San Jose that I knew. I texted him the picture from this shop in Jerusalem. It was great seeing a thriving skate scene there and a San
Jose connection.

On one of the last days of our trip, we visited the Peres Center for Peace and Innovation in Jafffa. Shimon Peres, the 91-year-old former prime minister and president of Israel and Nobel Peace Laureate, took time out of his day to sit down and talk with us. We got to hear words of wisdom from one of the country's founding fathers. He inspired me by sharing that his only regret is that he did not dream big enough. The conversation shifted to Peace Tech. Being a peacemaker was and is my passion. I tried to soak it all in and record the moment in my memory. It was the trip of a lifetime.

Meeting Shimon Peres at the Peres Center for Peace and Innovation in Jaffa, Israel

(April 2015)

A couple months later, the Latinosphere group was invited to speak at a tech conference in Guadalajara, Mexico called "Epicentro Fest." Speakers from all over the world came together to share ideas on how to create, transform, and build open cities that are full of knowledge.

My talk was titled "Beyond Technology, Keeping People Connected." It was an amazing experience meeting innovators and entrepreneurs during my four days in beautiful Guadalajara. I was so impressed with that city! It is a modern tech hub with high rise buildings, but it also maintains its traditional culture and history. Being part of Latinosphere and a guest of the Ministry of Innovation, Science and Technology, I again received incredible VIP treatment I didn't feel worthy of.

We were chauffeured around in the Jalisco governor's decked-out, bulletproof private bus. There were armed security following us in caravan. Just as Israel is a start-up nation, Guadalajara is a start-up city. We were taken to different incubators and "hacker garages" where I met super young, hipster engineers. I was blown away. This was a side of Mexico a lot of Americans never hear about. My perception of Mexico was totally expanded.

Meeting these enthusiastic engineers was inspiring. They were eager to tell us all about what they were working on in rapid Spanish. I listened to the interpreter but kept my eyes focused on them, caught up in their energy and expression. It made me feel very proud to be of Mexican heritage.

Our hosts surprised us with a helicopter ride from Guadalajara to Tequila. I was extremely nervous. I had never been in a helicopter before. I called my wife telling her I thought I should stay behind and not get on. My heart was pounding, and I was praying fervently. The other members of my group didn't seem to bat an eye. They were calm, cool, and collected. I gritted my teeth and tried not to be so obviously nervous as I kept wiping the sweat from my bald head. The Lord gave me a vision to pray over the city as I took in the gorgeous aerial view. I began to relax a little, but I couldn't wait to get home to hug my wife and kids.

We landed in a magical town. Tequila is literally one of Mexico's "Pueblos Majicos." I felt like I was in another world. It was so beautiful. We were given a tour and an extensive tequila tasting. I stuck to water, but I couldn't get enough of the food. It was prepared right in front of us with the freshest ingredients. Mexican food in Tequila, Mexico, now that was magical.

In 2016, I was invited to Baltimore, Maryland by the Office of Juvenile Justice and Delinquency Prevention and the Department of Justice for the annual Youth Violence Prevention Communities of Practice. On this trip, a group of pastors and church leaders were invited by Lt. Col. Melvin Russell, of the Baltimore police department, to the Sandtown-Winchester neighborhood. We went into the ground zero area where the Baltimore riots occurred over Freddie Gray, who sustained a fatal spinal cord injury in police custody.

As we walked through the streets people yelled out "the police killed Freddie Gray" and "no justice, no peace." I could physically feel the anger, pain, and hopelessness of this community. It was overwhelmingly emotional.

We had the opportunity to attend a small church in the very same neighborhood. We heard church leaders and young people share about their hopes for their community. They told us about what they are doing in their neighborhoods and how lives are being changed one person at a time. I had a heavy heart after hearing the chants from the streets of Baltimore, but in that moment, in that tiny church, I saw that there is hope.

In addition to Baltimore, there are many other neighborhoods in the United States with the same DNA: poverty, lack of quality education, drug pollution, and violence. Communities across our nation are experiencing similar pain and loss. Sometimes these neighborhoods explode, and they get national attention. Most of the time they implode, and our youth and children are left to deal with the aftermath. Often, they get little or no attention other than being known as "bad neighborhoods."

———————

Through some of my connections at the annual Silicon Valley Latino Leadership Summit and other organizations, I was asked to give the invocation at the HITEC (Hispanic IT Executive Council) in San Francisco. I was happy to see how generous and giving the organization is. I met some of the students and interns they were helping and felt really pumped to be in that environment with so many talented leaders.

My connection who had invited me there had heard about my story. He began introducing me and my wife to some of the prominent executives and decided to lead with, "Hey this guy's been stabbed!" Here I was standing in my tuxedo at this black-tie event. I couldn't even think of how to explain or what to say. Abby and I just stood there at a loss for words. The executive and his wife just stared back not knowing how to respond either. I felt like a fish out of water. We tried to get through the awkward silence, but it was pretty embarrassing. I wanted to be able to share my full story, but it's kind of hard when you're caught off guard like that.

This was all during cocktail hour, before it was time for me to get on stage and share the opening prayer. It wasn't the most confidence-boosting way to start the evening to say the least. I tried to settle my nerves before I had to address the huge crowd. When my host introduced me and read my bio, he added, "And he's been stabbed," just before I walked on stage. In the end, it all turned out well. I was able to thank some folks in the crowd by name, people who had personally donated laptops and resources to some of my students in need. God seemed to be showing me time and again that growth happens when we are out of our comfort zone. He carried me through another busy year of this amazing life.

Abby and me at HITEC Awards (October 2016)

CHAPTER 23

From Pain to Purpose, Purpose to Peace: Investing in the Now Generation

My quest through this life led me from pain to purpose to peace.

My life has come full circle. I even developed a relationship with law enforcement over the years, but I feel a strong urgency to see change and reform. I'm protective over my students. Kids will call me when they get pulled over and feel they're being profiled. I often get calls from students or parents looking for guidance after a bad run in with the cops. Tragically I've seen firsthand medical or mental health situations escalate to criminal situations or even death. There must be change.

For a long time, I kept myself extremely busy with my work. I was always going, trying to be there for everyone all the time. Some of my work is overwhelmingly dark, dealing with death and loss and seeing the pain some of the youth are facing. I've even lost some kids I was really close to through gang violence, hit and run accidents, and overdoses. I eventually had a bout of depression and anxiety that led to a relapse with alcohol.

I sought trauma-informed treatment that dealt with underlying issues and PTSD. When I first experienced my life transformation and came to the church, I tried to do all the right things and fit in with the church culture. There was an unspoken pressure to act like everything was fine, especially when I became a pastor. That didn't really allow me to face all the pain of my past, so it kept bubbling up. Things are much more complex than I could even imagine. There are layers upon layers, and recovery is a never-ending process. God wanted to take me to a deeper level of healing. I received Eye Movement Desensitization and Reprocessing (EMDR) and other forms of therapy.

Through treatment, I learned self-care, a totally new concept to me. I thought I could do it all, but I had to take a step back and care for myself in basic ways, like prayer, meditating on scripture, exercise, and taking walks with my family. We need to be gentle with ourselves. Healing takes time. Please be patient with yourself and with others.

The Bible tells us to meditate on these things:

"Whatever things are true, whatever things are noble, whatever things are just, whatever things are pure, whatever things are lovely, whatever things are of good report, if there is any virtue and if there is anything praiseworthy—meditate on these things. The things which you learned

and received and heard and saw in me, these do, and the God of peace will be with you" (Philippians 4:8–9).

We all experience pain in one way or another. Pain is real and can't be dismissed. I had to acknowledge my pain was real and be willing to expose it. For many years, I wanted to forget my past and what I went through. I didn't want to be seen as a messed-up, uneducated, ex-convict, but I couldn't stuff down the pain forever. I had to be me, and that allowed me to find my purpose in life. I can truly and fully identify with certain people in my community, in a way that other people never can. I do what I love and made it my career. I get to live out my passion in loving my community on a daily basis. I feel so blessed.

When I found my purpose and my calling, I then had to learn how to stop performing and earning. I had to stop being so busy and worrying if I had done enough. I do my best, but I can't stress. The outcome is in God's hand, and I trust things will work out. I can have peace even when I don't understand things.

"Be anxious for nothing, but in everything by prayer and supplication, with thanksgiving, let your requests be made known to God; and the peace of God, which surpasses all understanding, will guard your hearts and minds through Christ Jesus." Philippians 4:6–7

My quest through this life led me from pain to purpose to peace.

Having fun is the opposite of pain and trauma. Taking time for me or to just have fun isn't a bad thing. Skating is also my form of self-care. Doing what I love. I can head out to the skate park anytime I want, and I know I will see friends. Sometimes it's old homeboys from back in the day, sometimes it's little junior high students I work with, or other times it is some of my former students that I've watched grow up. I'll bring a case of water on hot days or buy a bunch of pizzas because I know they're all hungry. Jonah's constantly pulling at my arm to show me his latest trick. Skating with my son is a true joy.

What really helps most of all is maintaining a consistent routine of waking up early every morning to read my Bible and pray, like I did back in the beginning when I first got saved. I used to listen to hours of sermons on CD back then. Nowadays I listen to sermon podcasts and audiobooks. I came to truly understand that the Christian life is a life of rest. Rest is the highest form of faith. I used to be so concerned about what I was doing for God, when it was really about resting in what He had done for me.

I love the kids I work with. I love playing handball with them, taking them to new places, surprising them on their birthdays, going out to eat, watching them skate, or just making them feel special in some small way. Some of the best times are when I get to see them drop their guard and just relax and be kids. It's great seeing them just being silly kids, laughing and enjoying life.

In 2019, I initiated The Bandana Peace Movement, starting with our students and branching out to friends of The City Peace Project from all walks of life. Historically the bandana has served as both a positive and negative symbol. It has represented unity by symbolizing hard work, blood, sweat, and tears. It has also played a role in disunity by contributing to violent gang culture. Now more than ever we must seek peace—a powerful form of unity. The heart of The City Peace Project is pursuing a culture of peace that allows youth to thrive. We initiated The Bandana Peace Movement to invite all people into this mission of transforming our culture with a "Yes" to being a peacemaker. By receiving and wearing The City Peace Project bandana or bandana shirts, you are committing to a pledge of peace.

TheCityPeaceProject.org

Peacemaker Pledge:
I will build a peaceful, nonviolent community by committing to
Treat ALL others with love, dignity, and respect,
Seek peace between people, neighborhoods, cities, states, countries, and
the world,
Respectfully communicate with others,
Create an atmosphere of peace,
Treat others the way I want to be treated,
And I will love my neighbor.

The design resembles a classic bandana while incorporating meaningful symbolism. There are the checkers for Cali or a "checkered past," hands throwing up the peace sign, stars for direction, and hearts for love. The diamonds represent each person's individual value. The center heart has two intersecting arrows to represent the love we first receive, then that love and peace flow out to others and to our community. I later incorporated a rose design that represents blooming where you are planted.

Michal-Donna in her peacemaker shirt

When I decided to become a Christian at age 24 in jail, I wasn't ready to change or surrender. Later in life when I desperately needed a savior and cried out to God, I found the God who loves me. That decision to follow Jesus completely changed the entire course of life for all eternity. He has led me places beyond my wildest dreams. I found purpose and meaning. I found peace.

The culture I grew up in is completely foreign to many. When you see people exhibiting destructive behaviors and patterns, please realize there is something deeper going on below the surface. Let's come from a heart of love and strive for trauma-informed, holistic ways to address the problems we may see in our classrooms, neighborhoods, and communities.

My goal in sharing my story is to help those dealing with trauma and pain to know that there is hope. That trauma doesn't define us or determine our future. In fact, it actually makes us stronger. We can heal and use what we went through to help others. Please reach out for help and be easy on yourself. You can change your story. It's never too late.

"He who overcomes shall inherit all things, and I will be his God and he shall be My son."

Revelation 21:7

Here is the article listed on the White House website on 4/4/2012:

It is a privilege and an honor to serve my community and to be named a Champion of Change. I am an Assistant Pastor at Calvary Chapel San Jose, where for eight years I have had the opportunity to work with students, schools, recovering addicts, community service projects, and also families in times of loss. I presently serve as a community member of the Mayor's Gang Prevention Task Force among a remarkable team of dedicated men and women. In our current economy and times of limited resources, I am finding ways to unite and mobilize the faith-based community to reduce and respond to gang violence. To this end, I have partnered with the city to create a volunteer Community Chaplaincy First Response Program.

In a city of almost one million residents, it is important to see people as individuals and reach them on a personal level. After a gang-related homicide, a Community Chaplain meets with the family of the victim to aid in specific needs and reduce further violence or retaliation. We assist by listening, offering spiritual care as requested, arranging hot meals, and at times participating in funerals. All services are provided by the faith-based community on a volunteer basis on behalf of the city.

I have lived in San Jose, California my entire life, which makes this city and this cause dear to my heart. My wife and I have a blended family that includes five children, and almost all of our extended family resides here as well. I strive to keep San Jose one of the safest big cities for my family and others. My firsthand experience with gang culture and its repercussions allow me to connect and communicate openly with people in times of crisis.

I reached out and found help at my darkest hour, and that is one reason why I am working with a team to start a hospital-based intervention program. Community Chaplains will be part of a first response support system after someone has been injured in gang-related violence. It is important to reach the victim and family members while they are at a vulnerable crossroad and most likely to see the need to break away. This opportunity is fleeting, and if it is missed, the victim will often become further enmeshed in the gang through retaliation or bearing their injury as a badge of honor. It is critical to intervene in their lives immediately after the incident through a bedside visit.

Because of my past, I am all too aware of the dangers and consequences of gang activity, and I also know it is never too late to get out. My aim is to give hope to young people and help them to personally envision their life beyond their present experience. My faith in Jesus Christ drastically changed my life, and loving people in my church took the time to invest in me at a critical point. Now I am able to pass on the grace and hope that I have received to others in need. I believe that you should never give up on anyone or write them off as being a lost cause, because there is always hope for anyone who is willing to make a change of heart and direction.

Handing out Thanksgiving turkeys to families in need in 2020

Awards and Achievements:

Social Entrepreneur member of Latinosphere Tech International Delegation to Israel and Mexico

Commendation from Mayor Chuck Reed and the City of San Jose, 2012

Certificate of Special Congressional Recognition Service to Youth Awards Honoree by Member of Congress Michael Honda, 2012

San Jose Job Corps Service to Youth Award, 2012

Movers of Mountains Award Recipient 2013, The Dr. Martin Luther King Jr., Association of Santa Clara Valley

Community Bridge Builder, Gang Prevention and Intervention, Youth Advocacy by Dr. Martin Luther King Jr. Association of Santa Clara Valley, 2013

The City Peace Project received the "Compadres de la Comunidad" Award by MACSA in 2014.

Appointed as a Goodwill Ambassador for the Golden Rule International Award, 2015

Plaque of appreciation from Boys & Girls Clubs to Danny Sanchez for his support

Certificate of Recognition from California Legislature Assembly-member Nora Campos, 2015

Certificate of Recognition from Assembly-member Nora Campos and Senator Jim Beall

Certificate of Recognition from Assembly-member Nora Campos and Senator Jim Beall to The City Peace Project for service to the community

Commendation from the City of San Jose's Vice Mayor Rose Herrera to the Mayor's Gang Prevention Task Force-Community Engagement Subcommittee members including, Danny Sanchez, for their continued efforts in providing resources and solutions to prevent gang activities in our community, 2016

Certificate of Recognition from Councilmember Magdalena Carrasco, for commitment and service to the community of East San Jose, 2017

POST
traumatic
QUEST

Licenses & Certifications:

Parent Project Facilitator

Acute Stress, Grief and Trauma, Addiction and Recovery, Complex Trauma and Disaster, Crisis and First Responder, Domestic and Community Crisis Response, PTSD (Post Traumatic Stress Disorder) & Combat Stress Training by American Association of Christian Counselors

Thank You for Reading My Book!

I would love it if you would write a review and share my message, the quest from pain to purpose, to peace.

Thanks so much!

~ Danny Sanchez

PostTraumaticQuest.com
TheCityPeaceProject.org
Instagram: @TheCityPeaceProject
Instagram: @pastordanny_sanchez
Facebook: **Danny Sanchez**